DROVER

STARTUP GUIDE

#startupeverywhere

Startup Guide Lisbon

Editor: Jenna van Uden
Writer: Senay Boztas
Copyeditor: Laurence Currie-Clark

Art direction, design & layout by
Design Studio Maurice Redmond - Berlin
www.dsmr.berlin

Illustrations by sanjini.com

Lisbon Team
Project Catalyst: Ricardo Marvao
Project Manager: Edite Cruz
Photographers' Producer: Caroline Pullman
Photographers: Steve Stoer and
Pedro Pina Vasconcelos.

Additional photography by
Daniela Carducci, Celia Topping,
Filipe Penajoia, Camilo Gutierrez,
and Cristina Stoian.

Printed in Berlin, Germany by
Medialis-Offsetdruck GmbH
Heidelberger Str. 65, 12435 Berlin

Published by Startup Everywhere
Vestergade 82, 3 TV. Aarhus, Denmark
info@startupeverywhere.com

Visit: startupeverywhere.com

ISBN 978-87-93412-03-3

STARTUP GUIDE
LISBON

STARTUP GUIDE LISBON

In partnership with **Beta-i**

Proudly supported by

startup.focus.

Fernando Medina /
Mayor of Lisbon

Allow me to start by explaining the ambition and strategic vision that drives the work that we have been doing in Lisbon – transforming it into one of the most competitive, innovative and creative cities in Europe.

What has been happening in Lisbon is the result of a global strategy that brings together multiple actors to drive growth and innovation in a way that has never been done before. On one hand this strategy aims to attract and retain international investment, startups, corporates and talent, and on the other, to build a platform that brings together the right set of conditions to create and expand new ventures with Lisbon as a base. The local startup ecosystem is a thriving one, and this guide gives you a good overview of all that is happening here. The startups, founders, incubators, accelerators and experts who have been interviewed can help you create and grow your business from Lisbon. The directory can help you find who to contact and where to find them. In the past year we've had big news from the ecosystem: major international players opening offices in the city, startups publishing amazing success metrics, investment increasing, and new events and meetups popping up. Besides this, in the coming years we intend to turn the Beato Creative Hub into one of the leading entrepreneurship centers in Europe. All this comes to validate the energy and dynamism that is driving entrepreneurship in this city.

In 2015, Lisbon was the first city to be elected as European Capital of Entrepreneurship, and soon after that as host of Web Summit – considered the most important conference in Europe for digital and web technologies – for the following three years. All we have accomplished up until now fills us with pride, and we are considering it to be just the foundations of the future we are building. I invite you to use this Startup Guide as a tool to explore and build the future with us. Welcome to Lisbon!

Fernando Medina

[Overview] # Lisbon / Portugal

- **42%** of the total Portuguese scaleups were located in Lisbon (17 companies)

- **90%** of Portuguese scaleups were small, and raised **44%** of the total €160m capital raised (€1m–10m).

- 4 companies in the mid-scale segment secured the remaining **56%** of the total €160m capital raised in Portugal (€10–€50m)

- **65%** of the scaleups in the study had funding rounds in 2014 and 2015.

- There have been no Unicorns

- Software, business analytics and health drive the industry scaleup ecosystem of Portugal

- Cleantech, digital media and fashion are starting to attract more scaleups

- There have been 9 exits (M&A's) and no IPO's

- Fast country-wide broadband

Sources: startupeuropeclub.eu (Nov 2015), startupheatmap.eu

Founders would consider
starting up in Lisbon for
the following top reasons:

[Access to Talent]

5.2%

[Access to Capital]

3.7%

[Burn Rate]

3.7%

[Ecosystem]

5.5%

Lisbon

[Rank] # City Ranking

European founders had up to 5 votes
from a list of 30 cities

1. Berlin	6. Dublin
2. London	7. Stockholm
3. Amsterdam	8. Munich
4. Barcelona	9. Copenhagen
5. Lisbon	10. Vienna

STARTUP
GUIDE
LISBON

Local Community Partner

Beta-i

Fostering great ideas and watching entrepreneurs grow to their full potential is our passion. The startup world is changing; we challenge teams to embrace change, to take off their shoes, to make things happen. We challenge entrepreneurs to be the best they can be.

As the Portuguese innovation hub for integrated community-, startup- and corporate-based acceleration processes, Beta-i's mission is to improve entrepreneurship through three main acting principles: creating and boosting a network of entrepreneurship; accelerating startups with global ambition and facilitating their access to investment; and creating space, services and products focused on startups and their needs. Running in Lisbon since 2010, we've supported more than 500 startups, in over 40 acceleration programs, and had 93 startups invested, raising over €55 million.

Portugal has developed a significant number of world-class startups, incubators and programs, which have been key to the recent economic progress we've seen in the country. The great thing about Lisbon is the network of talented people who are always willing to help each other. It has been compared to San Francisco and to Berlin as one of the best cities in Europe to build a business.

Of course, there's always a downside – the fall-out of startups is hard to witness. Even founders with solid ideas and good business backgrounds sometimes don't make it. We have to accept this as part of the startup ecosystem.

That's why Beta-i believes we should play an essential role in bringing together startups and corporations, creating partnerships where both sides can benefit. This combined effort makes our commitment to continuous growth and international projection part of our startup ecosystem.
This guide is a good example of what all of us in Lisbon have achieved so far.

STARTUP GUIDE LISBON

startups

programs

Lisbon Essentials

A trading city that has always attracted tourists and sailed off with cultural prizes, Lisbon is now gaining a reputation as a great place to do and start business.

It was a different story in 2010, when Portugal requested a €78 billion bailout package from the IMF. But after a rocky recent political history, Portugal's 2015 socialist-led government is making the right noises about encouraging entrepreneurship. With a fair wind, it looks as though Portugal could be sailing back to its Renaissance days as a global trading powerhouse. It's a beautiful place to work, mixing World Heritage attractions like Jerónimos Monastery and Belém Tower, with quaint, quiet streets, the iconic 25 de Abril suspension bridge, and buzzing shopping/working/eating hubs like LX Factory. Lisbon City Council is building on a 2015 European Entrepreneurial Region of the Year award, with a rebooted innovation strategy.

To much excitement, the Web Summit tech conference begins the first of three 'editions' here in 2016, attracted by this Atlantic business hub allowing access to 750 million consumers, well-ranked universities and plenty of qualified, multi-lingual talent among its 2.8 million people. In a 2015 report, the Startup Europe Partnership said 40 startups have scaled up, raising €160 million in venture capital, nine successful companies have been bought, and Portugal's financial crisis years are behind: it is 'young but growing fast and well'. However, a Startup Manifesto compiled by local startup expert Beta-i suggests it's not all plain sailing: it cites limited local investment capital and calls for stable, globally-competitive taxes, lighter admin for startups and English as a mandatory language in everything foreigner-related. But if these clouds blow away, with its 270 days of annual sunshine, Lisbon's future looks bright.

Before You Come

Before you book your flight and pack your sunscreen, remember to do your research. The kind of visa[1] you can apply for depends on your own country's agreement with Portugal and the type of business you'll be setting up. Check with your embassy, the visa section and relevant government institutions. Best not turn up on a tourist visa and try to wing it, as you may have a less friendly relationship with the tax office further down the line.

Check that you'll have health insurance that will cover you while you get set up, you have the paperwork to prove who you are, and try to have enough in your bank account for six months' rent just in case you need to pay up front to convince a wary landlord – something that is not uncommon in countries with strong tenancy rights. Check whether you can stay with any of the shared work spaces that offer rooms, because meeting other startups might be a good way to finding a shared apartment. Better still, plan to start off lodging with a friend if that's an option. You should register with Iniciativa Lisboa as a resident as soon as you arrive.

Cost of Living

A beautiful teapot of mint tea in a sparklingly-clean café with decent internet will set you back... about 60 cents. The prices in Lisbon are surprisingly low (although wages are too). But this is a place to eat, drink, make merry and travel with abandon because even on a wage of €1,100 a month, you can live well. A train ride costs €1.40 and it's very easy to buy the 50 cent Via Viagem transport card which you simply load up, or buy a 30-day pass for about €35. Count on paying about €8 for a main meal in a restaurant, and more or less depending on the weight of your food if you use one of the canteens that stick your plate on the scales. Childcare costs are correspondingly low, and you might find it very affordable to have a live-in nanny or home help. Local products are cheap and good in supermarkets, although expect lots of strange-looking, tasty fruit and be aware that imported brands (such as nappies) may cost more than in larger countries.

Cultural Differences

In Lisbon, don't be surprised if people feel you're intruding if you arrive on time – or, God forbid – early. Or if in August the country partially shuts down and everybody goes on holiday. Portugal has a relaxed way of life, and a residual old-fashioned business culture. Do expect people to be consummately polite in person, respecting your personal space, dress choices and the queue for a morning espresso (*bica*) at the train station. The level of English, especially amongst young people, is excellent. But be aware that Portuguese is a lilting and long-winded tongue, and northern European directness may not go down well.

But on the bright side – and it being sunny Lisbon, there are lots of bright sides – people are incredibly kind and helpful when you're a stupid foreigner who is sitting waiting patiently for a metro train ... going in the completely wrong direction.

[1]Visa Help / See Government Offices page 203

Renting an Apartment

Apartments in and around Lisbon are both charming and charmingly cheap. You can get a bedroom somewhere in the city center for €300 a month and one-bedroom apartments at around €500 – a bargain compared to other European capitals. But the problem for outsiders, freelancers and startups is that most landlords demand a current work contract, and it can be hard to get an apartment without one. Try to exploit your network of friends to get started, meet other startups and see if there are informal shares available. Consider some of the working spaces where you can also stay, such as Startup Lisboa and the Surf Office. If you have some savings, you could offer six months of rent up front as a guarantee (or even buy something, with property prices low after the last crisis and incentives like golden visas for foreigners investing in larger houses). If all else fails while you're getting started, Airbnb brokers bedrooms from €25 a night.

See **Flat & Rentals** page 202

Finding a Co-Working Space

Lisbon is brimming with shared places to work, and it's a good idea to spend a day tramming, bussing, metroing and walking around the city to see which one best suits your vibe. Some have larger offices on offer, and you'll need to apply in advance due to high demand – for example, Startup Lisboa. Others are tiny and if you're a budding creative, working in a shipping container wedged next to a bus (at Village Underground Lisboa) might be just the thing to inspire you. Some places broker whole offices that you can fit out yourself (for example, Beta-i), while others have large attic spaces where a passing entrepreneur or two can fit in easily and cheaply (like CoworkLisboa or Lisbon Work Hub). If you're too cool for school, and rather richer, there will be something for you at Second Home, an outpost of the trendy London co-working place. Finally, the City of Lisbon is planning to create a massive co-work hothouse with something for everyone in a former military factory in the Marvila district ... so watch that space too.

See **Spaces** page 66

Insurance

Portugal has a national health system, and if you have a free European Health Insurance Card (which you can request as a member of another EU country), you are covered by reciprocal agreements. Otherwise, you'll definitely need your own health insurance, and you may want to consider this anyway. Decent jobs normally offer this as a perk for employees, and by setting up a company, you can access cheaper health insurance for yourself too. Investors will normally insist that you have life insurance, and of course you'll need proper cover if you are driving a vehicle (as many Lisbonites do – it's a car-driven city). It's worth investigating any free or cheaper insurances that come with credit cards and bank accounts, because these can be useful and save you money.

See **Insurance Companies** page 202

Visas and Work Permits

Since Portugal is part of the Schengen agreement, if you're an EU or European Economic Area citizen, you can freely live and work in Lisbon. The same applies if one of your family members is a Portuguese national. Otherwise, you'll need to apply for a long-stay visa for a temporary stay or residence from the Portuguese embassy in the country where you reside. There's also an attractive 'golden' visa permit program if you buy a house worth €500,000 or more, create 10 or more jobs, or transfer capital worth at least €1 million (plus several other options). This golden residence permit, introduced in 2012 to encourage foreign investment, allows you to live and work in Portugal and can also lead to citizenship. You don't actually have to be resident in Portugal for more than a week or two a year to qualify, but the investment needs to be there for five years. After this time you – and family members – can be naturalized. If you're outside Europe, creating a company can help you get an entrepreneur's visa: check with the SEF immigration and borders service, and your own country's embassy.

See **Government Offices** page 203

Starting a Company

There has been a political drive to reform old-fashioned company laws in Portugal, and there are also free government agencies (or investors) to guide you. First, you must get a fiscal number (NIF). If you're an EU citizen, you need to present proof of ID and a permanent address, which can be done via a virtual office provider. If you don't yet have a permanent Portuguese address or aren't an EU citizen, you'll need a fiscal representative to act on your behalf, and non-Portuguese documents must be translated and legalized. With your NIF number, the simplest option is the On-the-Spot Firm (*Empresa Na Hora*) scheme, allowing you to start your firm at a single office; there's also a *Portal da Empresa* to do this online if you're an EU citizen. With more complex company needs or a bigger budget, you can appoint a notary. Every company must nominate an accountant, and there's a list of government-approved ones available. If you're at all unsure, the free Invest Lisboa government service is always happy to help. Creating a business costs around €250, you need €1 or more in capital and all shareholders need NIF numbers, while accounting will cost from €50 a month.

See **Programs** page 52

Opening a Bank Account

Portugal uses euros and although you can draw cash from a foreign bank account in the country, your utility bills and taxes will be paid automatically from your local account, so it's wise to get one quickly (or bank with an institution that operates in Portugal too). Banks typically open early (8.30am until 3pm, Monday to Friday), you must be 18 and will have to bring your identity card, tax number, residency card and proof of residence to fill in various forms. If you want to open an account from abroad, you'll need to mail the application with a reference from your current bank, and put in around €250. The city is full of Multibancos ATM machines, and it's a good idea to have cash to pay for small things like bus fares and lunch. A lot of banking material is in Portuguese, although banks have an obligation to ensure you understand. Several banks have also failed recently. Beware of one unusually strict banking rule: if you write a check from a Portuguese bank without enough funds, you will be charged with fraud, fined 20 percent of the check's value, be blacklisted and banned from opening another bank account.

See **Banks** page 201

Taxes

Global accountancy firm PwC has called Portugal's tax offering 'Europe's best kept secret'. Its tax year follows the calendar year, and to register as a taxpayer, you need to fill out a registration form (*ficha de inscrição*) and take it to your local tax office before carrying out any taxable activity. With penalties from €200 to €2,500 for non-compliance, and rules around companies that are far from clear at first glance, you definitely need that accountant. As well as offering double taxation relief if you pay tax in other countries, Portugal has a 2020 scheme giving extra incentives to larger projects (with a minimum investment of €3m) on a case-by-case basis. Another scheme allows companies to deduct 150 percent of costs related to creating jobs for people up to thirty-five and the long-term unemployed, while capital gains in Portuguese companies held by non-resident firms are largely tax exempt. As far as personal tax goes, the rate for 'non-habitual residents in Portugal' is a flat 20 percent for employment, business and professional income for ten years – although normal citizens pay from 14 percent to 48 percent of income, depending on salary.

See **Accountants** page 201

Telephone Contracts

The major telecoms/multimedia businesses in Portugal are MEO, Vodafone and NOS and you can buy prepaid and contract SIM cards. To buy the former just go to a store with your identity document (which they may photocopy). For a contract, you'll need your Portuguese tax number and proof of address like a bank statement too. You can pay using the ATM Multibanco system, by dialing 1255 and visiting a shop, and also with direct debit for a contract. Mobile can be expensive, so many people rely on internet-based services like WhatsApp on their phones. Some resellers may offer better deals (such as Lycamobile and UZO) so ask around and do some research.

See **Phone Companies** page 203

Getting Around

Cheap, sparkling clean and pretty efficient, Lisbon's public transportation system passes with flying colours. Trains might sometimes be imprinted with beer adverts (including in dots over the windows) but they take you distances to the beach or into the quiet countryside on time and on budget. You can easily live with your family at the beach and take a daily half-hour train, or drive, into Lisbon city centre. Inside the city, the metro system is a little slow, but is well equipped with seats and coffee bars at the bigger junctions. Make sure you know the end destination of the direction you're going in so you choose the right platform. Buses take multiple routes and are very useful until rush hour in the city centre, when you'd be quicker walking. Trams are rattly but charming, although it's a small network. Meanwhile, when a hill gets really steep there's sometimes a handy funicular to take you up the slope so you can stay elegant and sweatless for your next appointment.

See **Public Transport** page 203

Learning the Language

As with anywhere you move, it's a good idea to learn the language: it's a way of better understanding its business life, and getting a competitive advantage. You may not ever speak Portuguese as well as the young generation speaks English, but at least you'll be polite and have a better idea of what's going on if a demanding letter arrives in Portuguese or you want to understand people chatting amongst themselves. Written Portuguese is intelligible if you speak Spanish or Italian, but because of the unique pronunciation, you will struggle to understand a word of spoken Portuguese without learning it – and it can even be hard to understand people pronouncing place names and foreign words. There are plenty of courses available and the prices are reasonable; CIAL, for instance, is a long-established school in Lisbon. If you've a basic proficiency, consider offering a language swap for conversation practice with someone in the startup community.

See **Language Schools** page 202

Meeting People

Shared office spaces – especially those with accommodation attached – are an obvious way to start building a network in Lisbon. All of the main accelerators and incubators offering offices and development programs for startups run meetings, sessions and talks, so go along to these. Many have active Facebook groups and online communities. As always, if moving to a new country, do all you can to learn the language and make time to pursue your own hobbies. If you like surfing, that's an obvious winner, and you can meet other surfer-entrepreneurs by staying and working at the Surf Office. When people go out, they tend to go to locations (such as Baixa-Chiado or Cais do Sodré) and bar hop, invitations to dinner tend to be last-minute and informal. There is a sense of safety, ease and family-friendliness that is the charm of the Lisbon lifestyle.

See **Expat Groups and Meetups** page 202

The Startup Guide Community
Join the global community for entrepreneurs, founders, startups, investors and enthusiasts. Find your local network, get feedback, and access talent, know-how and much more. Visit **startupeverywhere.com**

The Startup Guide App
Perfect navigational companion to the Startup Guide. Available on iOS and Android, featuring all the co-working spaces, incubators, accelerators and cafés with wifi, wherever you are.

ups

[Name]

EatTasty

[Elevator Pitch]

"EatTasty delivers authentic home-cooked food, wherever you are and whatever your cooking ability. Cooks just need to prepare the meals; customers just need to tap the app for local, homemade food at a competitive price."

[The Story]

Rui Costa and Orlando Lopes know one thing: they like a good meal. These keen eaters co-founded EatTasty, an app connecting home cooks like students and stay-at-home mums with office workers wanting quality lunches. The idea was born in August 2015, and won €75,000 in investment at the 2016 Lisbon Challenge accelerator, plus another €170,000 from other investors. Since then, EatTasty has employed an experienced chef to develop robust and tasty recipes, and recruited and fully trained its first four home cooks. 'EatTasty makes it possible to purchase from nearby cooks producing at home,' explains Lopes. 'They just need to cook, and can earn a secure salary.'

They have been running a trial phase with five companies nearby, offering a two-option menu via WhatsApp with main courses for €5.90 and drinks at €1.50. The cooks earn per meal and EatTasty supplies all ingredients and provides necessary kitchen equipment (possibly including a hire-purchase 'Bimby' robot cooker in future). It guarantees to buy and deliver all meals the 'home chefs' make, taking the risk of over-ordering. EatTasty's app and full website should launch in late 2016 and Costa advises similar startups: 'Think big, fail quickly.'

[Funding History]

Bootstrap   Seed Funding   Venture Capital

[Milestones]

- Getting the funding to employ a full-time, experienced chef
- Not waiting to develop a platform but starting WhatsApp trials immediately
- Refocusing on clients who want good food – and will pay for it
- Developing a consistent process we can replicate and scale

[Links]   Web: **eattasty.com** Twitter: **@EatTasty**

[Name]

Landing.jobs

[Elevator Pitch]

"We are a tech jobs marketplace: We match tech talent with employers."

[The Story]

There have been some bumps on the launch path for Landing.jobs. In May 2013, Portuguese computer science specialist Pedro Oliveira was asked if he knew someone to match tech talent at universities with roles. He volunteered himself, and José Paiva (his soon-to-be co-founder) joined him. Oliveira had worked on a last-minute travel booking system, which cost €30,000, and 'crashed and burned'. But Oliveira was determined. He and Paiva injected €50,000 of their cash, built and coded the platform, and started wooing clients from a space at Startup Lisboa.

The business launched in 2014 as 'Jobbox', which was confusing to say and even harder to spell. 'We dropped it,' says Oliveira. They also changed a revenue-splitting model for people recommending friends. Come February 2015, they raised €750,000 in venture capital from Portugal Ventures and LC Ventures and employed a rebranding service. They emerged a candidate-driven site called Landing.jobs, charging firms 11 percent of a recruit's year one gross salary. Landing.jobs operates from Brazil, Barcelona, Lisbon and London, focusing on Portugal, Spain, the UK, Germany and Ireland. Tools help candidates identify strengths and jobs, and the vision is to help techies build lifelong careers.

[Funding History]

Bootstrap

Venture Capital

[Milestones]

- Venture capital investment
- Paying €10,000 for rebranding
- First of the annual Landing.jobs festivals in July 2015
- Heading for profitability in 2016

[Links]   Web: landing.jobs Twitter: @landing_jobs Instagram: landing_jobs

33

[Name]

CoolFarm

[Elevator Pitch]

"A self-regulating system to grow plants sustainably in indoor farms and greenhouses. Sensors, machine learning and artificial intelligence technology help crops grow efficiently, giving them what they need when they need it, and the data is managed in the cloud."

[The Story]

Liliana Marques and João Igor are pretty chilled, which is fortunate because their CoolFarm smart indoor farming system is gathering some steam. In 2012, they started a website and mobile apps company called CoolApps(e) with co-founder Eduardo Esteves. Robotic engineer Gonçalo Cabrita – now CoolFarm CEO – was talking to Igor about the difficulties of growing healthy strawberries on his balcony, and they brainstormed around growing food using tech. 'We wanted to build a Nespresso-style machine just to grow plants, with a mobile app to control it,' explains Igor.

Investing about €50,000 from CoolApps(e), the four launched CoolFarm and went through the Lisbon Challenge program in 2014. It became clear that – fun as it might be to help backyard gardeners – it was indoor farm businesses that would pay for smart technology to optimize growing conditions. CoolFarm started looking for investors in Europe and the USA, eventually raising €1m from a Portuguese private equity funder, then almost the same again from Portuguese and European public funds. A team based mainly in Coimbra is developing the product, starting sales, and working with agricultural test partners. CoolFarm aims to launch its 'Plug&Play' system at trade shows worldwide.

[Funding History]

Bootstrap

Angel Investment

[Milestones]

- Finding the product idea, and accepting its market was businesses
- Getting the perfect team that believes in what we do
- Securing the right investment
- Getting test results back to 'prove the product value' and make sales

[Links]   Web: **coolfarm.com** Twitter: **@TheCoolFarm** Instagram: **thecoolfarm**

[Name]

Hole19

[Elevator Pitch]

"Hole19 connects you with your golf buddies, favorite golf courses and stats."

[The Story]

'The average golfer is shooting bogeys, including me,' admits Anthony Douglas, founder and chief executive of Hole19. So he has created an app to help these over-par golfers play better golf, while also aiming at a global sporting market worth billions annually. Douglas is half-American, half-Portuguese, speaks six languages and grew up in Austria. He tried to become a professional basketball player until he got injured, and so, back in 2007, he started the gentler game of golf. While working at Sony in Stockholm, he created personal 'dashboards' to improve his scores. He returned to Portugal in 2009, and two years later started mapping GPS distances throughout the country's golf courses.

Hole19 originally sold a paid-for app, then converted into a free model for golfers to research and rate courses, use GPS co-ordinates to plot shots and record their scores, and share experiences with others. It has had three rounds of investment so far, raising €1.9m, and recently launched a subscriber-only service. The app contains information on over 40,000 golf courses worldwide (in 14 languages), and has a million users, nearly 30 percent of them using it each month. 'Pick your team wisely, and treat them well,' Douglas advises other startups. 'And think global from the get-go.'

[Funding History]

Bootstrap

Venture Capital

[Milestones]

- Modifying the product to smartphones and smartwatches
- Increasing the team with each funding round
- Mapping the entire world: we should have scaled the business faster
- Focusing on people who know mobile, not raising money from the wrong investors

[Links]   Web: **hole19.com** Facebook: **hole19** Twitter: **@hole19golf**

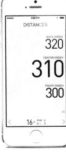

[Name] # Codacy

[Elevator Pitch] *"Codacy provides automated code review software that helps other companies optimise their software – rather like an extra developer on their team checking code, enforcing good practice and analysing security concerns."*

[The Story] In 2012, as part of his Lisbon-based master's degree in software engineering, Jaime Jorge started working on a code analysis business with his friend João Caxaria. 'We wanted to provide something on the cloud to correct code duplication, did a prototype called Qamine [quality assurance mine], and tried to sell it to the biggest telecoms companies in Lisbon,' says co-founder and chief executive Jorge. 'They used it but didn't pay for it. We learned a ton from customers on what they did not want, because that wasn't it.' In 2013, Jorge moved to London where Caxaria was working and they won a €50,000 investment from Seedcamp. They renamed to the simpler Codacy, and raised $500,000 to launch a built-in solution to improve all aspects of code quality that November.

'There's a bigger demand for developers than the supply,' says Jorge. 'A mid-level engineer in San Francisco costs up to $200,000 a year. Soon, every business will have some offering online and software will be integral to that. So you'll invest in tools that make the software development process more efficient, and that's where Codacy comes in.' With customers including Adobe, Codacy itself is now debugged and heading for profit.

[Funding History]

Bootstrap

Seed Funding

Venture Capital

[Milestones]
- Getting Seedcamp funding
- Our first paying customer, a German company (we still have the receipt)
- Our pre-seed funding round at the end of 2013.
- Hitting more than 200 customers at the start of 2016

[Links] Web: **codacy.com** Facebook: **codacy** Twitter: **@codacy**

Attentive

[Elevator Pitch]

"Attentive is a business intelligence tool that a company can add to its customer database. It delivers relevant, up-to-the-minute information about sales leads, competitors, partners and investors that sales teams can act on."

[The Story]

What if the contact you'd been nurturing for months suddenly changed jobs before signing your purchase order? Attentive offers a business intelligence tool that sales teams can plug into their customer database to alert them to multiple relevant changes – potentially making sales more effective. Daniel Araújo, chief executive, had the idea while working as an analyst for Google in London in 2014. 'I really felt the frustration of not knowing enough about my customers,' he says. 'We knew where information was being published but we didn't have time to look at it. I started looking for tools to help me do that but there wasn't one about my clients, connected to my customer relationship management database.'

So he started making one with his older brother, software developer Pedro Araújo (now chief technology officer), and friend Luis Miguel Braga, now chief operating officer. They quit their jobs, moved back to Portugal, took part in the Lisbon Challenge, and won €100,000 in Caixa Capital seed funding. The business now has companies testing its product, some customers paying a monthly subscription, and is raising €20,000 from four close advisors.

[Funding History]

Bootstrap   Angel Investment   Venture Capital

[Milestones]

- Dropping the idea of doing B2C software and focusing on businesses as customers
- Moving back to Portugal and doing the Lisbon Challenge[5]
- Getting investment, and focusing on fixing a problem people have
- The advisor round: we needed those guys on board to help us grow to success

[Links]   Web: **attentive.us** Facebook: **attentiveus** Twitter: **@attentiveus**

[Name]
Line Health

[Elevator Pitch]
"Our device will help chronic patients with multiple conditions take their medication. It will be given free to patients, who just need to insert their ready-organized monthly dose into the device to receive the right amount at the right time."

[The Story]
When Diogo Ortega's 85-year-old grandmother mistakenly took a pill meant for his grandfather, it meant a dash to hospital – and the birth of smart medicine dispenser Line Health. Ortega, now chief executive, developed a medicine reminder app for mobile phones during a 'hackathon' programming event, teaming up with Sofia Almeida – now chief operating officer – to do the Lisbon Challenge accelerator in 2014. They recruited two more co-founders, developer Luís Castro and product designer Joana Vieira. The pharmaceutical company Bayer invited them to its Berlin-based accelerator for four months, offering a €50,000 grant. They then began developing a smart pill dispenser and piloted it in Berlin.

At the end of 2015, they changed their original name of PharmAssistant to Line Health – simpler to write and more consumer friendly. They began operations in Boston, keeping software development in Lisbon, and raised $1m from investors. The prototype reminder and tracker device (which also alerts family members to problems) is being tested in American pilots, with the premise that insurance companies and hospitals will pay for them. 'Half of the medication that's prescribed in the world is not taken correctly, and the cost of this just in the US is $300bn a year,' says Ortega.

[Funding History]

Bootstrap   Seed Funding   Angel Investment   Venture Capital

[Milestones]
- Being coached by Bayer HealthCare's CMO at Bayer accelerator, Grants4Apps
- Realising we needed to develop a pill-dispensing product, not just a mobile app
- Changing the name from PharmAssistant, which had negative associations in the US
- Realising insurers and hospitals have an interest in paying for Line Health, although patients are the end users

[Links]   Web: **linehealth.com**   Facebook: **linehealth**   Twitter: **@line_health**

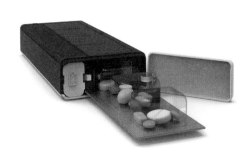

[Name] # Aptoide

[Elevator Pitch] *"Aptoide is a third-party Android app store, allowing customers to upload apps, as well as create their own stores to share them. Aptoide focuses on Southeast Asia and Latin America, where smartphone use is growing and Android is popular."*

[The Story] Aptoide started as a summer project in Paulo Trezentos' company, Caixa Mágica Software, in 2009. Together with Alvaro Amorim Pinto, who studied law but was always fascinated by technology, they created a platform hosting multiple app stores, and in 2011 Trezentos and Pinto co-founded Aptoide. By 2015, it had ninety-seven million users. Unlike Google Play or the Apple App Store, any user can create a store, rather like a YouTube channel. Aptoide's revenue comes mostly from adverts for Android applications and also a 25 percent commission on paid-for apps. It focuses on Asia, Latin America and the Middle East, where people often have no credit cards and so use its alternative payment methods.

Aptoide has raised more than $5m in investment and opened offices in Singapore and Shenzhen, China. But in 2014 it complained to the European Commission that it was 'struggling to survive', claiming Google pushed users away from stores rivalling Google Play. This antitrust investigation was formalized by the EC in April 2016 and COO Pinto says: 'the complaint was necessary to make sure the Android market continues to be open [with] space for new companies to provide innovative products and services. Let's see what the future holds.'

[Funding History]

Seed Funding   Venture Capital

[Milestones]
- Taking Aptoide from a side project to launching the platform
- Closing the seed round, to grow faster
- Deciding to look for investors and customers outside the US and Europe
- Keeping the pace in terms of growth, against larger competitors

[Links] Web: **aptoide.com** Facebook: **aptoide** Twitter: **@aptoide** Instagram: **@aptoide**

45

[Name]

Science4you

[Elevator Pitch]

"Science4you focuses on the development and commercialisation of scientific and educational toys. Its vision is to develop society's educational standards by developing toys and games that enable children to learn about several subjects while playing, in a simple, pleasant and intuitive way."

[The Story]

Science4you's chief executive has a favourite toy in its educational range: the volcano. 'People love explosions,' says Miguel Pina Martins. Appropriately, the business he founded as a graduate in 2008 should smash €80m in 2016 sales. The award-winning firm operates in Portugal, Spain, Italy, France and the UK, selling smart toys to enthusiastic parents in more than 18 countries. It has a smartphone for children and products ranging from a T-Rex wooden puzzle to a 'DNA Detective: Criminal Investigation' set.

Leaving Lisbon business school, Martins started with €1,000 of his own cash and €45,000 from investors. 'We thought people were looking for education and there was a good possibility of making toys that enabled kids to learn,' he says. 'It's mixing two trends: education and fun, which will always be a trend with kids.' With venture capital funding and increasing annual sales, Science4you built a factory and head office in Loures, north of Lisbon. Martins says this location is an advantage. 'Labour is not that expensive, and there are highly qualified and committed people.' Science4you has 200 people working in the factory, 100 in product development, and 200 in shops. But the entrepreneur – awarded the Portuguese order of business merit in 2015 – warns a startup isn't child's play: 'Work, work, work,' he says. 'Don't get lost.'

[Funding History]

Bootstrap   Angel Investment   Venture Capital

[Milestones]
- Building a factory
- Winning collaborations with the University of Lisbon, Scientific Park of Madrid and Oxford University
- Recruiting industry expert John Harper, former chief executive of Hasbro Europe
- The first international sale in 2014

[Links]   Web: **science4youtoys.com** Facebook: **Science4youUK** Twitter: **@Science4you_UK**

[Name] # Talkdesk

[Elevator Pitch] *"Talkdesk is a cloud-based call centre software that helps companies connect with customers in real time to increase customer satisfaction and loyalty."*

[The Story] "Until now call centres were complex to set up, difficult to use and required a fortune," says Tiago Paiva, founder and CEO. So, to solve this problem, Paiva created Talkdesk, a cloud-based call centre software that's easy to use, costs one-third of the regular price, and takes just minutes to set up. What started off as a fifteen day prototype for a startup competition ended up having a valuation of hundreds of millions of dollars.

Paiva has avoided the spotlight of being a successful entrepreneur over the past few years. Considered by Forbes as one of the most talented people under thirty, he grew up in Portugal, learned how to code at 15, and then stopped coding one year after he graduated. Not long after the idea of Talkdesk popped up, a prototype was created and the team headed off to San Francisco.

Since then, Talkdesk has received an overall investment of $24.4m and has developed integrations with Salesforce, Zendesk and Shopify. Currently, Talkdesk has offices in 56 countries, including Lisbon, Chicago and San Francisco, but Tiago keeps raising the bar: 'Our goal is to go public'.

[Funding History]

| Bootstrap | Seed Funding | Angel Investment | Venture Capital |

[Milestones]
- Raised our seed round of funding and hit $1m in ARR
- Established an office in the US and started to build the team there
- Grew from 20 to 100 employees
- Won our first million dollar contract

[Links] Web: **talkdesk.com** Facebook: **Talkdesk** Twitter: **@talkdesk**

[Name]
Tradiio

[Elevator Pitch]

"Tradiio allows music creators to set up a subscription page where their fans can support them on a monthly basis in exchange for access to exclusives, unique rewards and experiences. The platform blends crowdfunding and music streaming with the mission of generating recurring funding for musicians."

[The Story]

Álvaro Gomez left strategic consultancy to co-found a music tech startup in 2013 with Exago Ventures, Tradiio's first promoter. They co-invested €100,000 and, after recruiting Miguel Leite from Universal Music Group as chief marketing officer and Andre Moniz as CTO from Betfair, they launched in 2014.

Tradiio (fusing 'trading' and 'radio') started as a game. Musicians uploaded music, and listeners betted on acts to win points. The startup also scouted for acts and took a percentage of record label deals. With €1.8m in total investment from ESV, it participated in a Microsoft accelerator and launched in the UK. But despite having 250,000 listening members and 20,000 musicians from Portugal, Brazil, the US and UK, the artists were not making money. So Tradiio pivoted to a free streaming platform where artists offer extra subscriber-only services, like dedicated content and free tickets. This artist's subscription model started in April 2016. Forty percent of artists participated and 10 percent started earning, some up to €1800 a month for musicians like Adam Bomb (a New York based rock singer and guitarist). 'Artists used to have 10,000 fans and make €10 in streaming a month,' says Gomez. 'This lets them leave the coffee job and work in their craft.' Next stop: America.

[Funding History]

Bootstrap   Seed Funding   Venture Capital

[Milestones]

- Finding a cause

- Building a team passionate for music and tech

- Learning by launching in the UK market.

- The 'reality shake': realising we weren't making money

[Links] Web: **tradiio.com/artists** Facebook: **tradiio** Twitter: **@tradiio** Instagram: **tradiio**

- **Don't start alone: Build a team.**

  'We lost Ronaldo in the first 20 minutes [of the Portugal vs France Euro 2016 football final],' says Marquet. 'Everyone said without him we are nothing. They proved they are a team, and are resilient.' Your first sale is selling the product idea to potential co-founders.

- **Lean startup method.**

  Prototype and test your product as much as you can before committing the money. Test it on friendly users first.

- **Test your co-founders.**

  Go and live and work together for two weeks, and it will be obvious if it's going to work out.

- **You need over €100,000 to launch a physical product**

  Tap into funds, angels, private investors, crowd funding and – if you have a high-tech innovation – venture capital. Don't forget businesses that might use your product. Companies that are already in the market might need, and fund, innovation.

Productized

[Name]

[Elevator Pitch] *"We are the one-stop-shop to make your product idea come to life by providing mentors, experts, lab facilities and a network within the Portuguese manufacturing industry."*

[Sector] **Product Management, Hardware and Digital Startups on Medical technology, IoT, Robotics, Defense and Clean Technology**

[Description] Productized is a registered non-profit focusing on product-based startups, founded in 2015. It runs startup accelerator programs for hardware products, helping people develop ideas into working prototypes. Its clients are mostly young students from the 'gold mine' of research institutes and universities around Lisbon, although it's open to anybody. It also runs talks, weekends, boot camps and the Productized annual conference.

The products it supports involve 10 percent hardware, 90 percent software, and it wants to get them from thesis to minimum viable product (as the jargon goes) to allow thorough testing. Productized also runs a roadshow to market its services to technical universities and institutes, encouraging the shyest 'lab rats' to bring their ideas to life. It has, for example, helped Norwegian PhD researcher Annelene Dahl develop a baby-monitoring t-shirt, the Hugo Bear, through a weekend boot camp. These allowed her to meet electronic board and materials manufacturers, plus potential funders, to make a t-shirt responding to a baby's temperature, heart rate and skin moisture levels to alert parents or activate baby-soothing recordings. A smart gas tank monitoring product, NESTO, has potential Asian investment thanks to exposure via Productized. It also helped students develop the Inpack (Portuguese for 'great'), a backpack that converts into a shopping trolley.

Ten projects are selected for the annual Productize.it boot camp week, with a €50 engagement fee. The winner gets a €5,000 prize with no strings attached, and there's €2,000 for second and €1,000 for third. 'In most of these projects the starting point is different from what they end up developing,' says André Marquet, president of Productized. He advises young startups to go to a startup accelerator with an open mind, protect their intellectual property, and find the right partner: 'Start young,' he says. 'Energy is more important than experience. It's a very difficult game and your partners are going to mean a lot. Hardware is hard.'

[Apply to] André Marquet / andre@productized.co

- **Don't find your co-founders in a bar**
  They need a business mentality. Have an
  intellectually honest conversation with them
  to ensure your goals are aligned.

- **Think about the soft side**
  Choosing your team and building a culture is
  groundwork for a good business.

- **Don't force the idea**
  You don't look for an idea: it finds you.
  But don't find solutions to things that aren't
  problems either. Fit your product to the market.

- **You have to be really focused and
  drill down everything**
  Obsession is great, but don't lock everything out.
  Be balanced and resilient too.

- **Timing: look forward**
  Apps are a mature market now, while AR and VR
  (augmented and virtual reality) are at the
  beginning. Bear in mind you might be too early
  for a market.

- **You can't control luck**

[Name]

Lisbon Challenge

[Elevator Pitch] *"We run a three-month, intensive accelerator program focused on helping founders build their roadmap to product-market fit, and fundraising on Demo Day. Forty percent of our 160 alumni have raised investment, with a total of $52m."*

[Sector] **Technology**

[Description] Lisbon Challenge is a three-month acceleration program that helps founders build their roadmap to product-market fit and fundraise at Demo Day. Founded in 2013 by Beta-i, it currently runs twice a year, targeting early stage tech startups that are transitioning from prototype to product MVP. Being an intensive founder-centric program, it requires at least two co-founders to attend and one of them must be responsible for the technological part. Startups referred are given priority, and once accepted, all international teams get a €1,000 grant for relocation costs.

The programs cover four main topics, crucial for the setup of any startup: 1) understanding the real customer segment pains in first hand, 2) building or improving the product to better fit those customer segment needs, 3) applying the first go-to market strategies and growing those metrics, and 4) fundraising at Demo Day. All of these topics are what Lisbon Challenge considers essential to build a solid roadmap for product-market fit, and they are all delivered in different sessions ranging from workshops, to mentoring, and frameworks.

Recent 'alumnus' Impraise, a co-worker feedback tool, raised $1.6 million in funding, and others have gone on to world-renowned seed funding programs Y Combinator, 500 Startups, Techstars and Seedcamp. The Fall'16 Lisbon Challenge was scheduled for September, at the time of a major technology conference, Web Summit, in Lisbon. Nuno Machado Lopes, managing director and a forty-six-year-old entrepreneur himself, says: 'We are founder centric, working with founders on their inner self and interactions. You don't see that in many accelerators, but relationships and lack of alignment are reasons many startups fail. It's an irrational thing creating a startup. You have better odds in a casino.' He recommends that startups should define where they are headed, and only go to an accelerator program if it's a good match: 'Three months in a startup's life is an eternity and they must ensure they're ready and don't have false expectations. Investment can never be guaranteed.'

[Apply to] Nuno Machado Lopes / nuno.lopes@beta-i.pt

[Links] Web: **lisbon-challenge.com** Facebook: **LisbonChallenge** Twitter: **@LisbonChallenge**

- **Be as honest as possible**
  Say up front 'these are the elephants in the room' and funders who believe in you will help you address these issues.

- **Identify the unknowns**
  What's the competition? What's the cost of growth? How much does it cost to acquire one customer and what is that customer's long-term value?

- **Decide on your funding model**
  'What business can we build around your technology?' asks Amorim. 'Is it a multi-billion dollar company, or a niche market, VC fundable or not? Not everything will be fundable by venture capital – thank God! It's for a unique opportunity that's going to explode. But it is hard work, and a very violent process.

- **Be absolutely obsessed with success**
  'From what I see from the top achievers, it's a necessity,' says Amorim. 'If you don't have the drive, it's too easy to give up, to be tired of earning no salary, losing your partner, and fighting against all odds. You have to be obstinate – in a nice way.'

Building Global Innovators

[Name]

[Elevator Pitch] *"Building Global Innovators (BGI) is a three-month accelerator for later-stage, technology-based startups with solid teams in place. Most have a prototype ready to pilot, and they receive mentoring, training and connections to investors. If the startup is successful, BGI takes 3 percent of equity."*

[Sector] **Technology**

[Description] A decade ago, the Portuguese government pledged €300m to a project fostering scientific collaborations with five international universities, including the Massachusetts Institute of Technology (MIT). 'The component they were missing was a model to take ideas for commercialization, translating research into jobs or the next Google for Portugal,' explains Gonçalo Amorim. To fill this gap, he was asked to launch Building Global Innovators (BGI) as part of the MIT Portugal Program at the University Institute of Lisbon business school (ISCTE). 'Historically, Portugal hasn't been a cutting-edge research country, but Mariano Gago [former minister for science technology and higher education] said we needed impact,' says Amorim. 'All this investment needed to convert to something, making technology-based businesses paying higher salaries. Startups then were being born, and dying in incubators. VCs were telling us the problem wasn't creating companies, but that they would never explode, becoming prisoners of European funding, service companies, or losing the edge.'

In 2010, he launched BGI as a competition for up to €1m in Caixa Capital investment for four winners per year. In 2013, it became a full-blown business accelerator, and now the annual program selects ten to twelve international startups. These applicants work intensively for a week-long 'boot camp' with sixty experts who give one-to-one advice on pitches, business plans and relevant regulatory affairs. The last day of this week is a semi-formal pitch and Q&A with potential investors. Then the potential firms have ten weeks to work on an eighteen-month business blueprint, with weekly meetings with BGI. The program is sponsored by CGD and linked with investment from Caixa Capital and around fifty other investors, and it takes 3 percent equity in companies that get to a first round of investment with a €2m valuation. (Otherwise, the program – which claims to provide in-kind services worth €1m – is free). BGI has worked with 117 new companies, which have raised €80m in funding, created 450 jobs – and, most importantly, over two-thirds are still going.

[Apply to] Gonçalo Amorim executive director / geral@bgi.pt

[Links] Web: **bgi.pt** Facebook: **Building Global Innovators** Twitter: **@MITPortugal**

- **Join the community**
  Don't be afraid to share your idea and talk about lessons learned along the way.

- **Listen**
  'An entrepreneur's ego is the main reason for startups to fail: when you understand another person is giving you constructive advice, in your interest, that's a piece of advice you want to consider,' says Rita Lucena.

- **At the same time, be crazily confident in yourself**
  Find the right balance.

- **Consider your funding model**
  Just because you have raised funding, that doesn't mean you'll succeed. 'Doing it in a bootstrap way is better, because you aren't wasting anyone else's money or giving up equity,' says Rita Lucena.

- **Scalable business is the way to go**
  Fábrica de Startups is looking for ideas without borders.

FastStart

[Name]

[Elevator Pitch]
"Fábrica de Startups works with all kinds of people, from those who want to start up but don't have an idea to groups of four with a prototype. It uses its nine-step FastStart methodology to get them to pitching stage."

[Sector]
Tourism, energy, health, banking, retail

[Description]
Fábrica de Startups – literally the 'factory of startups' in Portuguese – is a business running eight free programs a year to help people develop entrepreneurial proposals. The FastStart nine-step system involves developing a business model, testing whether it really works for a market and is valuable enough for people to buy, then planning financing and execution before pitching it to potential funders. Its simplest programs are 'ideation' weeks, aimed at solo wannabe entrepreneurs who wish to find their idea. Sometimes these are held only in Portuguese, the costs are funded by business sponsors and about 150 people from all kinds of backgrounds apply for the 50 places. They are put into teams and first work on analyzing an industry. On the second day, they get out and about to do interviews or surveys, and the third is spent building a solution for the problem they have found. The fourth day involves making a detailed business model, and the fifth is pitching day.

'We had applications from very varied people, students, middle-aged, unemployed, people tired of working wherever they were working and ready to take a week of vacation to try something new,' says Rita Lucena, acceleration manager. Each week has a different sponsor and focuses on a relevant industry. Summer of startups is a month-long program aimed at university students in all disciplines. There are 'bootcamp' intensive sessions twice weekly at CATÓLICA-LISBON business school, aiming to help them develop theses into potential companies. Meanwhile, for teams of three or four entrepreneurs ready to test an idea, the business offers four-week FastStart programs (free of charge and with no equity taken). Selected teams from all of these programs can win investment plus six months of free office space. Fábrica de Startups successes include WeRoll, a social networking group for people to share series of pictures that tell a story, like an old roll of camera film.

[Apply to]
Apply via the website: **fabricadestartups.co/programs**

[Links]
fabricadestartups.com Twitter: **@FabricaDeStartups** Instagram: **fabrica_de_startups**

- **Taking the first step is half the battle**
  'There are scores of brilliant ideas out there, hampered by people who think they aren't good enough, don't have the money or are afraid of the risk,' says Queiró. 'Just get started!'

- **Building a strong team is the smartest thing you can do, but don't overthink it**
  You don't need 100 people to get that idea off the ground; you probably need three, but if you choose the right three, your chances will rocket.

- **Don't take too long in getting your product out to sale**
  'People will forgive you for early mishaps,' says Queiró. 'Pokémon Go has higher average revenues per user than Facebook but it crashes every five minutes. It doesn't do three-quarters of what it should, yet they are making €1m a day. A minimum viable product is better than nothing!'

- **Don't be afraid of feedback**
  People can get very defensive because their idea is their baby: take it as a learning opportunity.

Acredita Portugal

[Name]

[Elevator Pitch] *"Portugal's largest entrepreneurship school, running an annual competition for anyone with a potential business idea related to the country: if you want to do something, fancy or not, we will take you in and give you the tools to succeed."*

[Sector] **Portuguese Entrepreneurship**

[Description] From tubes of artisanal jam to an oral cancer detector, Acredita Portugal helps bring a rainbow of business ideas to life. Founded in 2008, this sponsorship-funded organization has a simple goal: to get people creating companies. Its first entrepreneurship competition in 2010 had 706 applicants for thirty places, and since then it has trained 130,000 people in building projects which have raised €5m in investment. Some 19,000 people apply each year for the free program, with ideas from homemade nut butters to a cutting-edge hair salon (now Slash Creative Hair Studio). Selected wannabe entrepreneurs are trained in the business skills to develop a minimum viable product, with dedicated volunteer mentors and a board of advisors. The companies judged to have the strongest prototypes by April join a two-month acceleration program of weekly sessions to help them find clients, partners, investors and start making sales. The winners get €100,000 in investment (in exchange for equity), plus advice services valued at €1m.

'Eight years ago, Portugal was a rather depressing place,' explains thirty-year-old chief executive Pedro Queiró. 'There were no startups, no Unbabel, Feedzai, Uniplaces, and many youngsters' dream job was to join a government agency. Our goal is to give an opportunity to everyone, regardless of experience and background. People may not be high-powered engineers, but we believe there's a lot of potential: maybe not the next Uber, but a café with great burgers or store making amazing beach towels.'
Queiró says that there are some barriers in the legal structures required to create a company, and the 'complexity' of using equity as compensation in Portugal.
But there are great advantages: 'Right now, Portugal is cheap, we have an amazing infrastructure and a lifestyle you can't beat. Between Beta-i, Acredita Portugal and Startup Lisboa, just here in Lisbon you can cover any need, from the lowliest idea to the most sophisticated startup trying to scale across the world.'

[Apply to] **geral@acreditaportugal.pt**

[Links] acreditaportugal.pt Facebook: acreditaportugal Twitter: @AcreditaPt

- Find a problem to solve, rather than cool things to do

- Come up with a relevant solution and focus on a market.

- Make sure you are making money.
  Invoice rather than seek funding. 'It's not cool: it's tough,' says Duarte. 'You will have time with no money; you have to fire your best friend. People don't always tell the real story. They're in Forbes Magazine. A couple of years after, they're bankrupt.'

- Work on the human side of the business, team and culture, or it won't be sustainable.

- Don't get caught up in the startup universe
  'I call it the egosystem,' says Duarte. 'Forget about the egosystem. If you go to Porto, they are focused on producing revenues and delivering. They don't go to parties with beer and pizza and all-night coding.'

- Hire people who fit your culture, not for their CVs

Big Smart Cities

[Name]

[Elevator Pitch] *"Big Smart Cities is a competition for startups working on technology to improve life for people visiting, living, studying and working in cities. We help with a broad range of ideas: apps, sensors, open data and devices like urban furniture."*

[Sector] **Smart cities technology**

[Description] Can't find a space to leave your car on the bumper-to-bumper streets? A winning startup from Big Smart Cities might have the answer. The 'pre-acceleration' program helps startups with a tech-based idea or prototype they want to develop, and its 2016 champion Parkly is all about helping drivers find city parking.

The part-time annual program lasts eight weeks, with training and mentoring from experts including sponsors Vodafone, Ericsson, Microsoft and Celfocus. Participants end up with a pitch, plus a functional prototype or end product to demonstrate. More than 200 teams apply and 20 are selected as finalists. There's no fee, and the workshops take place during the weekend so that everyone can join. Week one has a kick-off session, there are one-day workshops in the third and fourth weeks, then after intensive training in pitching, it's demo day. The competition has around twenty judges including sponsors, academics, investors and people from other organizations working with startups.

Winners get a €10,000 prize with no strings attached or equity taken. They also receive free office space at the Vodafone incubator for six months to a year and Vodafone's help in finding a route to market. Organizer Miguel Muñoz Duarte stresses the focus is on getting people to develop something that others want to buy, and making money. 'My opinion is that we are living in a bubble,' says Duarte, also a professor of entrepreneurship at Nova School of Business and Economics. 'The message we in the ecosystem, the media and even professors pass to people is not the right one. We care too much about fame, Silicon Valley wannabes and hype. What's important in business? Revenues, invoicing, controlling costs, and having a service that's relevant. I always recommend to our startups: don't raise money. Make your business sustainable by itself, then if you want to accelerate, perhaps you want investors.'

[Apply to] via the webform at **bigsmartcities.com**

[Links] Web: **bigsmartcities.com** Facebook: **BIGsmartcities** Twitter: **@BIGsmartcities**

ces

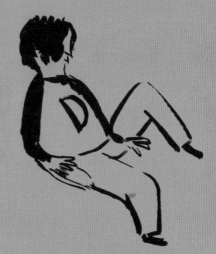

Village Underground Lisboa

[Name]

[Address] Museu da Carris (Carris Museum of public transport), Estação de Santo Amaro,
R. 1º de Maio 103, 1300-472 Lisbon

[Transport] **Tram:** 18E, 15E **Bus:** 714, 727, 732, 742, 751, 756, 720, 738, 760

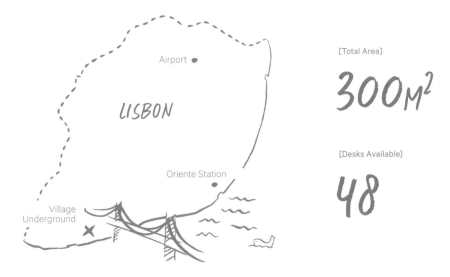

[Total Area]

300M²

[Desks Available]

48

[The Story] Two multi-colored buses perch atop fourteen shipping containers like children's building blocks. This isn't a toy: it's a shared office space. The co-founding manager Mariana Duarte Silva from Portugal was following her dreams at Village Underground in London, managing DJs from a shared working space/arts venue in recycled underground train carriages. But in 2009, she headed back to Portugal to start a new life. 'I asked the founder of the London project, Tom Foxcroft, if he wanted to do it in other cities,' she says. 'He's an adventurer and crazy like I am, and said: why not?'

With help from a new Lisbon municipality innovation department, a bank loan and €30,000 in sponsorship, she spent €250,000 transforming a rented space at the Carris transport depot in regenerating Alcântara into Village Underground Lisboa. Today she lets desks in twelve containers to creatives, self-confessed geeks, a theater company and a bikini shop. It's €150 a month for a turn-up-and-go desk (€500 for a container), including air-conditioning, cleaning and internet. 'Residents' get discounts at the fragrant canteen-in-a-bus, the swing, the skate park, and weekend events, plus a free birthday party. 'The most important thing is sharing ideas with like-minded people and not being stuck in your apartment,' says Silva. 'Here, people can be inspired.'

[Links] Web: **vulisboa.com** Facebook: **villageundergroundlisboa** Instagram: **@village_underground_lisboa**

Face of the Space:
Mariana Duarte Silva, is co-founder/
manager of Village Underground Lisboa,
a job that she calls a 'life project'.
Infectiously energetic, she organizes a
year-round calendar of music, events,
arts and entertainment and keeps her
residents happy. That means everything
from booking in corporate events for
Mercedes and L'Oréal and organizing the
twice-yearly Cargo street food market, to
finding the right IKEA night-light for one
tortured writer.

[Name] # Beta-i

[Address] Avenida Casal Ribeiro 28, 1000-092, Lisbon, Portugal.

[Transport] **Metro station:** Saldanha or Picoas

Airport ●

LISBON

Beta-i ✕ ● Oriente Station

[Total Area]

2,150м²

[Desks Available]

400+

[The Story] The CTT postal services office in central Lisbon used to be a stamp collectors' paradise. After years of semi-abandonment when most of the firm moved out, it is slowly acquiring a new collection of tenants: startup businesses. Six of the ten floors are currently managed by Beta-i, a support organization for Lisbon startups, which is gradually renovating, subleasing offices and brokering tenancies. Beta-i itself sits mainly on the second floor, a stripped-back space with tiled floors, industrially-bare ceilings, chipboard partitions and colourful furniture donated by sponsors or given in part exchange for services. Desk space is sometimes rented to 'entrepreneurs in residence', and also used for startup accelerator programs like the Lisbon Challenge.

Other floors in the 6,000 m² building are let to firms from accelerator successes (such as Attentive.us) to accountants. Like a stamp collection, the building has a pick 'n' mix feel. Some floors have been modernized (like the colourful auditorium on the eighth floor), others await renovation, with relics of out-dated office space meeting a bright, young, DIY vibe. The second-floor kitchen and sunny, smoker-friendly balcony are communal, and Beta-i co-founder Tiago Pinto has cost-cautious plans to make a restaurant and lounge on the first floor.

[Links] Web: **beta-i.pt** Facebook: **beta.i.pt** Instagram: **beta_i**

Face of the Space:

Tiago Pinto, 42, from Lisbon, is co-founder and head of money and people at Beta-i. This association sees itself as a connection for startups in this ecosystem in Portugal. The business tagline – 'ready when you are' – is in English, reinforcing the international mindset and culture of the organization, and it connects businesses with investment, runs accelerator programs and offers entrepreneurs space, events and services.

[Name] # Coworklisboa

[Address] Rua Rodrigues Faria 103, LX Factory, main building, fourth floor, 1300-501 Lisbon

[Transport] **Metro Station:** Alcantara-Mar **Bus:** 201, 712, 714, 720, 727, 732, 738, 742, 751, 760

[Total Area]

800M²

[Desks Available]

65+

[The Story] Tiago Figueiredo apparently felt a little shy when he started working in the cavernous shared office at Coworklisboa. So the photographer decided to take a portrait of everyone there including Buddy Batata, the resident dog. A year-and-a-half later, this series still hangs along one side of the shabby-chic space, on the top floor of an old fabric-making factory.

This attic for 'freelancers, nomads and businesses', includes variously-sized rooms, a café with a view and a curious layer of plastic ceiling insulation, for heat- and leak-proofing. More than 750 people have worked here since it opened in 2010, and Coworklisboa has partnerships with similar outfits, the Mutinerie in Paris, betahaus in Berlin and Templo in Rio de Janeiro.

A flex desk costs €100 a month, and this is a rare spot where you can easily turn up for a day (€12) or a week (€40). A fixed desk will set you back €150–€180 a month depending on size, and people just wanting a seat in the lounge and internet access pay €50 monthly. Coworklisboa also offers sets of desks for teams, by-the-hour meeting rooms, and a free trial day. Meanwhile, just outside, LX Factory is bursting at the seams with trendy shops.

[Links] Web: **coworklisboa.pt** Facebook: **Coworklisboalx** Instagram: **coworklisboa**

Face of the Space:
Fernando Mendes, 48, Coworklisboa
founder, found the perfect home for this
lively, shared workspace. 'LX Factory
is very special in the way that it is self-
organized,' he says. 'Mainside [the landlord]
doesn't have an office here. That means
there's a high level of freedom. No other
place in Lisbon has this very special set up,
and LX Factory worked as our marketing
plan. There's a lot here besides working!'

[Name] # Startup Campus

[Address] Rua Rodrigo da Fonseca 11, 1250-189, Lisbon

[Transport] **Metro Station:** Rato or Avenida **Bus:** 706, 709, 720, 727, 738, 773, 774

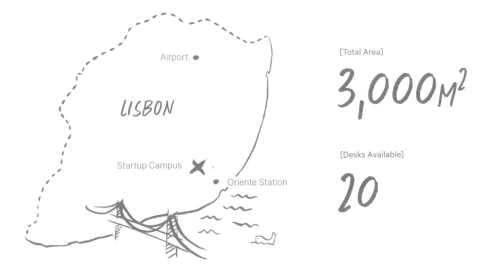

[Total Area]

3,000м²

[Desks Available]

20

[The Story] 'Live your dreams,' says a breezy banner across the front of Startup Campus. Through the doors, which cunningly open to your call only if your phone is registered on the system, is a warren of rooms over six floors. Here, industrious bunnies tap away in artificially-lit corridors, coming up for air on the sunny rooftop terrace.

At one of Portugal's leading shared workspaces, a desk costs from €35 plus VAT per month. The basic package allows twenty hours of weekly access to 'flexible desks' on the ground floor, including the use of meeting rooms and a well-equipped kitchen. Twenty-four hour access costs €75 plus VAT monthly, and for a dedicated desk, it's €100 plus VAT. Other floors and offices are let by larger startup businesses. Residents enjoy weekly events such as an entrepreneurs' breakfast, founders' lunches, practice 'demo nights' and rooftop socials. An area on the first floor becomes a stage with 150 seats, and there are also two floors of car parking space.

The vibe in the former bank is clean but spartan, with white office ceilings, laminate floors and the odd brightly-coloured chair. But, as successful startup residents attest, this affordable, functional space helps make dreams concrete realities.

[Links] Web: fabricadestartups.co Facebook: FabricaDeStartups Twitter: @FabricaStartups

Face of the Space:

António Lucena de Faria, founder and chief executive of Fábrica de Startups which operates the Startup Campus, says he likes the space because of its feeling of community. 'It is peer level sharing,' he says. 'I particularly believe in the close mentoring of people that are only a few months ahead of you and what you are doing as a startup.'

[Name]
Mouraria Creative Hub

[Address]   Rua dos Lagares 23, 1100-022 Lisbon

[Transport]   **Metro Station:** Martim Moniz **Bus:** 12E, 28E, 734

LISBON

Airport

Mouraria Creative Hub

Oriente Station

[Total Area]

1,400m²

[Desks Available]

40

[The Story]   Mouraria Creative Hub sits on fertile soil. When the building was renovated in 2014 thanks to a €2m grant from the European Union, excavators found fragments of beautifully-painted tiles and hand-crafted pots from the public baths that used to sit there. Today, these twelfth to fifteenth century artefacts are on display in the white-walled entrance corridor.

There's a quietly industrious feel to the place, which is called the Mouraria 'innovation center' in Portuguese. The labyrinth of odd-shaped office spaces on its three floors is home to creative industry workers including a milliner, material designer, video makers and a chef. It is equipped with solid wood floors, a kitchen support, function room and terrace, printers, sewing machines, and a sense of calm out of the hot Lisbon sun.

The space opened in May 2015, with an open call for people to apply to 'incubate' their businesses there using the working space as well as accessing its mentors and training. Currently, contracts are from six months to four years, although the City of Lisbon project may soon offer shorter stints. A desk, available 24/7, costs €100 per month plus VAT, and there are discounts for teams of up to four.

[Links]   Web: cm-lisboa.pt/en/mouraria-creative-hub Facebook: **Mouraria Creative Hub**

Face of the Space:
Carla Sancho, the forty-two-year-old executive co-ordinator, has worked for the City of Lisbon for more than a decade and jumped at the chance to move to Mouraria. 'It's very boring to sit at a desk,' she says. 'I like event production, to sit with them, facilitate projects, and I have a passion for music. I've tried all my life to bring interesting people to the city.'

[Name]	# The Surf Office
[Address]	Rua de São Paulo 111, 2nd floor, 1200-275 Lisbon
[Transport]	**Train Station:** Cais do Sodré **Bus:** 25E, 202, 714, 758, 774

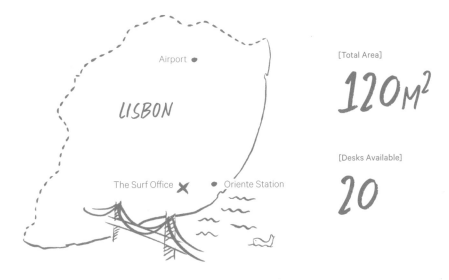

[Total Area]

120M²

[Desks Available]

20

[The Story] Like a quiet wave, you need to slip past a little store and up a couple of flights of stairs to lap at the door of the Surf Office. This relaxed work and living space in the heart of Lisbon is easy to overlook – there's no sign on the door, and although the ground floor kiosk staff will nod you towards a staircase, it doesn't look promising – at first.

Actually, up on the second floor is an elegant apartment of two offices, a meeting room and kitchen, with twelve bedrooms above. If your application is accepted, for about €60 a day you can use this as a base to work, sleep and then – if you like – head for Lisbon's surf too. (The only signs of the surfing residents, though, are a sunny dress code and boards leaning casually against the walls).

Slovakian web designer Peter Fabor established the stay-work-play concept in the Canary Islands, where he moved to in 2013, and opened the second Surf Office in Lisbon a year ago. He's fully booked, perhaps with the help of features in The New York Times, BBC and The Guardian, and is raising funding to open in other beautiful, windy places around the world.

KEEP

ROCKING

Face of the Space:
Peter Fabor, 30, seems as laid back
as his space – although there's a smart
business mind behind the T-shirt and
shorts. 'Surf Office is for professionals
who can work remotely and want to live
in Lisbon for one or two weeks,' he says.
'It's the kind of place you want to be if you
visit a place, and need to work and travel
alone if you don't have a social network.'

Startup Lisboa

[Name]

[Address] Rua da Prata 80-81, 1100-420, Lisbon

[Transport] **Metro Station:** Cais do Sodré or Baixa-Chiado **Bus:** 15E, 25E, 28E, 206, 207, 208, 210, 706, 711, 714, 728, 732, 735, 736, 737, 746, 759, 760, 774, 781, 782, 783

[Total Area]

1,500M²

[Desks Available]

200

[The Story] Blackboard walls, AstroTurf carpet and blue sky views in the 'thinking' room at Startup Lisboa hint at a municipal project with a difference. Back in 2011, Lisbon municipality had allocated cash for a 'participatory budget', the public voted on what to do with it, and one result was the private but non-profit association, Startup Lisboa. So far 250 startup companies have used this business incubator's office and mentoring facilities (via application), providing an estimated 1,000 jobs – while former director general João Vasconcelos has become Portuguese secretary of state for industry.

Today, the venture includes a six-storey building of variously-sized offices, a shared kitchen, lounge, and an eating space. It has a second building for bigger startups opposite, a residence for entrepreneurs with fourteen bedrooms to rent nearby (CASA Startup Lisboa) and a commercial business center at Lisbon airport. Encouragingly, its hard-working housekeepers are recognised online as part of the team. Currently, forty-seven companies are physical residents, renting offices from €100 to €300 a month (depending on size) and another fifty-three have €30 a month plus VAT 'virtual' membership, with access to mentoring plus pro bono legal and consultancy services. The organization has a program of events to help accelerate its fledgling businesses' development, and introduces them to potential funders.

[Links] Web: **startuplisboa.com** Facebook: **startuplisboa** Instagram: **startup_lisboa**

Face of the Space:

Miguel Fontes, the forty-five-year-old chief executive, says: 'What the startup's value is the flexibility and agility we offer here. We can answer different needs for different startups, although we focus on tourism, commerce and tech. They range from social economy to digital literacy businesses. Meanwhile, Lisbon is in the right position to support startups, with good talent, a cosmopolitan environment and a very appealing cost of living.'

Liberdade 229

[Name]

[Address]   Avenida da Liberdade 229, 2nd floor 1250-142 Lisboa Portugal

[Transport]   **Metro Station:** Marquês de Pombal

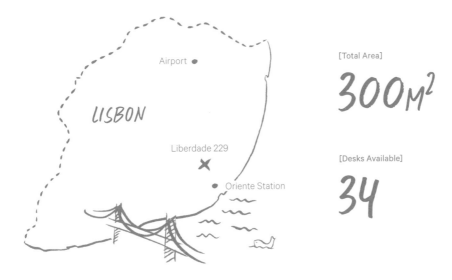

[Total Area]

300M²

[Desks Available]

34

[The Story]   Tupperware pots do more than spill out of drawers in the kitchen of shared workspace Liberdade 229: they line the whole of one kitchen wall. This tongue-in-cheek artwork is a remnant of the floor's chief tenant, Leo Xavier, who decided to rent out desks back in 2009. Xavier's company Quodis had been floor-sharing with another business, which moved out. Now he is away in London and long-term tenant Daniel da Silva is office manager. Liberdade 229 is a beautifully-preserved former apartment on the city's well-connected 'Champs Elysees', the Avenida da Liberdade.

On the second floor, via stairs or an old-style lift, are seven work rooms, a well-equipped kitchen and a meeting room with table tennis and television – handy for weekly winter movie sessions. The wide desks and decent chairs are livened up by Xavier's art, including red, topographical maps of Lisbon carved in layers of MDF and an eight-pronged chandelier. Designers, developers, traders, typographers and a Portuguese journalist pay €180 a month plus VAT for 24/7 access to a desk. The minimum time one can rent is one month and there's no maximum. 'I like the environment and the people who work here,' says Silva. 'We do a lot of things outside the office, and lately just three desks have been free.'

Face of the Space:
Daniel da Silva, office manager and a web developer for one tenant, Development Seed, was born in Switzerland and is half-Portuguese, half-Italian. He fits perfectly into the professional, multilingual vibe at Liberdade 229, where people quietly get on with business, interrupted only by a decent coffee or quick game of ping pong.

[Name]
Lisbon Innovation Kluster

[Address] Rua Braamcamp 88, 5th floor, 1250-052 Lisbon

[Transport] **Metro station:** Rato or Marquês de Pombal **Bus:** 706, 709, 720, 727, 738, 773, 774

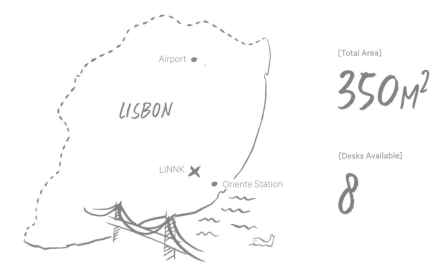

[Total Area]

350M²

[Desks Available]

8

[The Story] From the picture of Albert Einstein on the meeting room wall to the 'superheroes corridor' featuring images of Mr Spock and Yoda, LINNK's office has an eclectic mix of occupants. Based on the top floor of a classic, 1910 wooden-floored building in Lisbon's most expensive business district, this shared office was founded when startup consultancy META ICG relocated from Boston in 2014.

Joana Rafael, co-founder, says: 'When the Portuguese startup industry started booming, we created a space where META would have the right facilities to work in technology – a meeting space, a lab, a workspace in a premium location – and shared it with other startups. When you start up, sharing experience and networks is very positive.' The clean, high-ceilinged office has balconies with views, a sun room, kitchen, plus offices with large whiteboards. A bespoke meeting table incorporates a touchscreen monitor and legs like a pile of Jenga blocks. Today META partners with companies and startups to develop their tech products and IoT solutions, offering its services and space for entrepreneurs' meetups.

[Links]   Web: **linnk.us/meta-icg.com** Facebook: **linnk.us** Twitter: **@LINNK_US**

Face of the Space:

Vasco Portugal and Joana Rafael love
the vibe of the space, with its excellent
equipment, plus guitars, paintings and
a massive teddy bear. "It's very cosy,'
Rafael says. 'We have really good design
and an environment that's good to work in.
You don't feel tired, even if you're in
the office for hours.'

Lisbon WorkHub

[Name]

[Address] Rua Amorim 2, 1950-022 Lisbon

[Transport] **Bus:** 210, 718, 728, 755, 781, 782

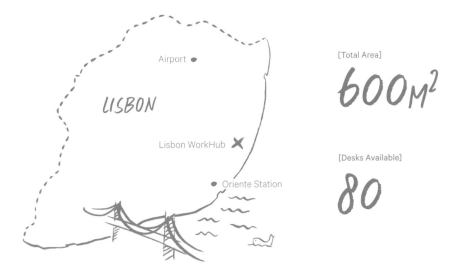

[Total Area]

600м²

[Desks Available]

80

[The Story] A century ago, Lisbon WorkHub was owned by winemakers, its high ceilings testament to a rich trade. The building was designed by a prized architect in 1910, and wealthy merchants lived in two apartments inside the building. But when Sara de Praetere opened the cobwebbed doors in 2014, it had been abandoned for three decades to pigeons, rats and damp. De Praetere enlisted her architect mother and €150,000 in private investment for an award-winning renovation.

Today, Lisbon WorkHub contains small offices for serious entrepreneurs, the attic is a well-ventilated shared working space, and there's a large events room costing up to €500 a day for everything from yoga classes to filming. What was originally a patio joining the buildings is now a smart but relaxed reception and lounge.

A desk here costs €120 plus VAT per month, and a whole office is €500 plus VAT. There's a free day's trial – although book in advance as it's running at 80 percent occupancy – and free parking. 'People like it because the space is different from traditional offices, full of glass and metal and low ceilings,' says De Praetere. 'We introduce everybody, and notice a lot of people working together.'

[Links] Web: **lisbonworkhub.pt** Facebook: **lxworkhub**

Face of the Space:
Sara de Praetere, the 31-year-old founder and chief executive, comes from Lisbon. She opened the offices in July 2015 in the once run-down neighbourhood of Marvila, which developers have now earmarked as a hot spot. She has also founded a monthly Portuguese publication on new businesses, called StartUp Magazine.

Olivier Grémillon / Airbnb

Managing Director - EMEA

Founded in August of 2008 and based in San Francisco, California, Airbnb is a trusted community marketplace for people to list, discover, and book unique accommodation around the world – online or from a mobile phone or tablet. Whether an apartment for a night, a castle for a week or a villa for a month, Airbnb connects people to unique travel experiences, at any price point, in more than 34,000 cities and 191 countries. And with world-class customer service and a growing community of users, Airbnb is the easiest way for people to monetize their extra space and showcase it to an audience of millions.

What are the most important steps for creating a successful online marketplace?
Airbnb believes, from its experience, that it's very important to get to know your community. Only when their challenges and where they come from are understood, can you really grasp what their needs are. And Airbnb has learned that this knowledge only comes from engaging with them. At Airbnb, the best part of our job is engaging with our community, whether it is at a small local meet-up or at Airbnb Open – an annual gathering in November where Airbnb celebrates with thousands of hosts from around the world. This year, we're hosting our biggest Airbnb Open yet, in Los Angeles. It will be three inspirational days of talks, performances and conversations.

What can startups do for their cities on a local level, and what's your relationship to the city?
It's very important to approach each and every city individually. Every city has their own set of amazing assets, differences and quirks, so it's important to go local and really understand what the city and its people are all about. Airbnb works very hard to get to know its local host community, engaging directly with them in meet-ups, and always welcoming feedback, comments and suggestions.

Do & Don't:

Do get to know your community.
Do things that don't scale.
Do your best to simplify procedures.

Don't forget to listen to your community.
Don't be afraid of failing.
Don't lose focus.

 ## 3 steps each startup should take, from idea to scale-up:

- Test things, even if they don't seem scalable.
- Collect all the knowledge you can about your product or service.
- Optimize your business plan.

Airbnb is all about innovation and creativity, so it also tries to connect with the local startup community. Since 2014, Airbnb has been active here in Lisbon supporting activities like the Lisbon Challenge Tourism Day to help grow the local startup scene.

Airbnb´s relationship with the city of Lisbon has been an incredibly positive one. Lisboners are known to be very open, so it's no surprise that the concept of home sharing has taken off. Just in 2015, the Airbnb community hosted 450,000 guests and contributed €268 million in economic activity in Lisbon. Airbnb has a partnership with the Lisbon Municipality to promote responsible homesharing, and to simplify the payment of tourist tax for hosts. The new tourism tax process, which began on 1 May 2016, is fully automated and allows Airbnb to collect and remit tourist taxes from guests on behalf of hosts.

How can startups manage fast growth?

Being agile and entrepreneurial is fundamental, both in the early days and when the business experiences rapid growth. Airbnb is invested in making sure every employee feels empowered to innovate. One of Airbnb´s mottos is 'embrace the adventure', which is key when you're in the business of building new things.

It's very important that startups always keep in mind their core values, and make decisions based on them. This will allow them to focus on the goals and the mission, while always keeping in mind what makes the company unique.

How can a small business build a strong team culture?

Reiterating what I mentioned before: solid core values. It's paramount to hire team members that share the company core values. At Airbnb, we have cross-functional interviews to evaluate if a candidate reflects or has the potential to reflect our core values. This is a crucial step in the hiring process to make sure only people who will preserve and add to the culture are hired.

It's also very important to celebrate the differences between team members and their individuality. The more diverse your team is, the higher the chance you get to develop innovative solutions.

Airbnb´s workspaces are designed with meeting rooms that replicate real Airbnb listings to inspire those in the room, and with different shared environments for our employees to work in. Culture is about more than having fun at work, it's about creating an environment for people to do their best. Just this year, Airbnb was thrilled to be named Glassdoor's #1 Best Place to Work.

[Links]   Web: **airbnb.com** Twitter: **@airbnb** Instagram: **airbnb**

"It is essential to get to know our community. Only when we understand their challenges and where they come from, can we really grasp what their needs are."

Luís Roquette Geraldes & Vasco Stilwell d'Andrade / MLGTS

Coordinators of Team Genesis

Morais Leitão, Galvão Teles, Soares da Silva & Associados (MLGTS) is an independent full service law firm with over 190 lawyers working in three offices in Portugal. Through MLGTS Legal Circle and anchored in our alliances with local leading law firms, we have access to legal services in Mozambique, Angola and Macau. The firm is also the exclusive member in Portugal of Lex Mundi, the world's leading network of independent law firms, present in 100+ countries worldwide and with more than 21,000 lawyers around the world – all from a single point of contact, allowing us to seamlessly handle our clients' most challenging cross-border transactions and disputes.

In early 2013, following up on know-how gathered over several years and based on the desire to foster and help national ventures thrive and scale internationally, Team Genesis was officially set up. The members are focused on "bet the company" transactions and high-value advice for scalable startups, whether acting for the founders or the investors. The team is extremely active and experienced in national and international investment rounds and exits, notably equity rounds (seed and preferred rounds), convertible notes (or convertible equity), venture debt and trade sales (including acqui-hires). We have been advising national and international investors and startups active in fintech, biotech, medtech, big data, legaltech, infratech, gaming, SaaS, consumer services, food delivery, and more. We also advise on IP (protection and commercialization), tax and estate planning, non-dilutive funding, visas and labour matters, founders' agreements, incorporation and flips to other jurisdictions, employee stock option plans, be it physical or virtual (phantom or stock appreciation rights), partnerships and joint-ventures, and agency/distribution agreements.

Team Genesis was the only team focusing on emerging companies to be commended in the 2015 Financial Times European Innovative Lawyers Awards (in both "business development" and "client service" categories).

Do & Don't:

Do understand the investor's business.
Do your homework.
Do accept the investor will want to control their investment.

Don't ignore the legal paperwork.
Don't underestimate how time-consuming fundraising can be.
Don't over dilute founders in early rounds.

 3 steps each startup should take, from idea to scale-up:

- Protect IP properly.

- Retain decent advisors early on.

- Seek proper legal advice before scaling.

What legal knowledge should a founder know before starting up?

Being a founder is not an easy craft. Here are some of the most crucial matters for a founder to know before embarking on a new venture:

- **Protecting IP** – you would be amazed at how much "clean-up" work lawyers have to do when it comes to intellectual property. It is most likely one of the few assets of the startup, and yet entrepreneurs who are careful enough to ensure all IP is properly assigned to the company are a rare sight.

- **Founders' agreements and why they differ from the by-laws** – this topic intertwines with the previous one. More often than not founders have blurred ideas and misconceptions about how corporate bodies interrelate, but also (and even more blatantly) about how by-laws differ from shareholders' agreements.

- **Vesting** – every founder should know what vesting is and should embrace it as a best practice which protects everyone involved in the project.

- **Becoming acquainted with stock option plans** – be it while bootstrapping or when closing the first funding, you should acknowledge that you will have to give up equity in order to retain talent at early stages.

- **Winding up** – you should always be in a position where you can immediately wind up the company if need be. For that to happen, you need to make sure you can settle all debts, especially the ones owed to the tax authorities and social security.

What are the best corporate forms to start up in and why?

As a rule of thumb, you should always choose a limited liability company. In Portugal you have two types of limited liability companies: private and public. The best corporate form for you to start with would be a private limited liability company for a number of reasons:

- Close to zero capital requirements
- Very light governance structure
- Relatively low running costs
- Restrictions on share transfers are easy to implement
- It can always be transformed into a public company if/when a preferred financing by an institutional investor occurs.

In general, there is no legal reason why you should not start with the private company because it can always be transformed into a public company thereafter (provided the requirements are met, notably, minimum share capital). In this country, unlike what happens in the US, you will not face dreadful legal and tax consequences if you happen to choose an inadequate corporate form.

The only scenario where you can envisage using another corporate form (i.e., a public company as opposed to a private company) is one where there is a legal obligation to do so as it is often the case with fintech startups where the applicable laws and regulations require a minimum share capital or a particular corporate form. Lastly, and this is true for the majority of cases, incorporating a company in Portugal is rather straightforward, cheap and hard to get wrong.

How does one go about creating a 'founders and shareholders agreement'?

When thinking about a founders' agreement, you should focus on the equity split between founders, the vesting schedule, good/bad leaver provisions, IP assignments and restrictive covenants (exclusivity and non-compete). Experience tells us that when you think about such an agreement you immediately think about three to five main topics, but if we were to sit down and ask a few initial questions, the topics would rapidly increase. When thinking about a Shareholders' Agreement with an investor and in addition to the foregoing, you should be primarily focusing on the structure of the investment (equity/debt, tranches, milestones and dilution), understanding cap tables, veto rights, exits and liquidity enhancement mechanisms. It is sometimes shocking to see how people lose track of how the cap table stands at any given moment, particularly when you start stacking up convertible notes with different conversion triggers/valuations and stock option pools. The same should be said for how little founders typically know about the impact preferred shares and liquidation preferences have on the (asymmetric) distribution of proceeds in an exit scenario. Founders' agreements (and shareholders' agreements in general) can be very complex legal documents which are not to be taken lightly. You should seek proper legal advice in order to make sure you fully understand what you are signing up for and whether what is intended is properly reflected in the wording of the agreement.

What are some great housekeeping tips for staying organized?

- Make sure all founders and employees assign the relevant intellectual property to the company

- Have proper labour agreements in place, notably, containing confidentiality undertakings as well as restrictive covenants (to the fullest extent legally admissible)

- Have a founders' agreement in place with, at least, the provisions discussed above

- Maintain a tight control on how the cap table stands and how the proceeds in an exit would be distributed amongst the shareholders

- Monitor how much of your stock option plan you have already used up (always look at your cap table on a fully diluted basis)

- Keep your ledgers and minutes books updated and in good order

- Maintain proper record of all the contractual arrangements entered into – it will come in handy sooner rather than later

- Keep track of the relevant metrics to your business

- Maintain sound accounting practices

Good housekeeping will make your life that much easier. It will facilitate and expedite fundraising. And it will allow you to sleep better at night if you can claim your company is in absolute pristine condition when entering into an investment agreement containing several pages of representations and warranties. Further, having the records of the company in good order will impress prospective investors and portrait the founders as a trustworthy team which, ultimately, is probably the most vital factor for an investor to decide to invest.

[Links]   Web: **mlgts.pt**

"
Sophisticated and savy entrepreneurs are legally astute. They know that preventive lawyering ultimately reduces overall legal fees. "

Paulo Soeiro de Carvalho / Lisbon City Council

General Director for Economy and Innovation

Five years ago, the mayor of Lisbon created Portugal's first city directorate-general (DG) focused on building its economy, encouraging investment, innovation and entrepreneurship. Today that long-serving mayor, António Costa, is Portuguese prime minister and the innovation DG connects up a little universe of bright focal points across Lisbon.

Paulo Soeiro de Carvalho, general director for economy and innovation, has built up a DG that led to the city winning a European Entrepreneurial Region of the Year award as an 'Atlantic business hub and gateway to the Americas, Africa and the EU' in 2015. The prize jury particularly highlighted the initiative Empresa Na Hora ('company time'), allowing people to set up a business quickly, the city's Startup Lisboa incubator, Lisbon Challenge accelerator program and its youth entrepreneurship program. Meanwhile, Lisbon will host the technology conference, Web Summit, from 2016–2018, with the help of around €1m in public investment and campaigning from the active startup 'ecosystem' that it now supports.

The DG for Economy and Innovation has a staff of seventy people spread through different projects and programs, and a budget of around €500,000 a year (plus access to other pots of investment cash) to make Lisbon 'one of the most competitive, creative and innovative cities in Europe.' In 2012, the flagship Startup Lisboa incubator was founded as the result of the city's innovative participatory budget, for which citizens propose and vote on ideas. The DG began working with universities to encourage international and business links, and attract investment and companies (using the city agency Invest Lisboa for these purposes). Today, there's an 'incubator network' of fifteen sites where early-stage companies can work and learn. The city promotes and supports accelerator programs (such as its own Smart Open Lisboa, inviting companies to do things with open data), FabLab Lisboa, which is the city fabrication laboratory and makerspace, and more than forty co-working spaces. On top of this, it fosters a network of investors including the government-backed Portugal Ventures, and the city's crowdfunding platform BOABOA.

How does the city hall help local businesses start up?

We have a one-stop-shop for every company that comes to the city. If they are very small, they can come to Iniciativa Lisboa, which has all the information they need. If they are bigger and want different facilities, or to know about fiscal and labour incentives or office spaces, they can go to Invest Lisboa.

In terms of helping people develop a business, the city has several initiatives, (including the micro-entrepreneurship Lisboa Empreende – winner of the European Enterprise Promotion Awards of the European Commission) and is partner in a number of incubator and accelerator programs: Startup Lisboa is the first and most prominent. In the creative industries, it supports Mouraria Creative Hub. Meanwhile, its FabLab Lisboa aims to give anyone access to the tools they need to invent 'almost anything', with the help of milling machines, laser and vinyl cutters, a 3D printer and high-powered computers. Anyone can book the equipment; there are also special workshops for young people aged sixteen to twenty-five called the Young Creators Program. Finally, the city can plug into a new package at a national level, Startup Portugal, a government entrepreneurship strategy giving access to fiscal and labour-related incentives for larger businesses.

If you are a startup, you also have a network of accelerators, incubators, investors, business angels, venture capital firms and different spaces thriving in Lisbon, and the city can guide you to the right ones for you. Explore the ecosystem and talk with the right people because some of the decisions you will take about locating (or relocating) in Lisbon will revolve around finding the best kind of space, mentorship and services. Consider also listing your idea on the BOABOA crowdfunding site supported by the city (boaboa.pt). Current projects seeking cash there include the thirty-three students behind Técnico Solar Boat who want to build a solar-powered boat to take part in international races and LDFA – Little Dresses for Africa Portugal, which makes clothing for vulnerable children.

How does the city hall help build a network for startups?

We work to bring together big companies and startups. At 'startup meet-ups', we invite fifty startups and seventeen companies and investors for fifteen-minute conversations. The city of Lisbon puts out a call to people in its startup ecosystem – as we call it – to ask if they want to meet companies like Cisco, SONAE or Deloitte. We've had two so far and want to run this event three times a year, because this kind of access can be invaluable for an early-stage company.

"We want to be one of Europe's most creative, innovative cities and anyone who wants to join that dream is very welcome."

3 steps each startup should take, from idea to scale-up:

- Think global.

- Get very strong mentors.

- Be flexible: things are changing very fast and you will need to change to adapt.

Do & Don't:

Do talk with the right people.

Do be flexible and agile.

Do work very fast and be ambitious.

Don't go to a bank in the beginning; figure out different ways of getting investment.

Don't think local, think global.

Don't doubt Lisbon! Even if it's small, our startups are big.

The publicly-supported accelerator Building Global Innovators – based at the Higher Institute of Business and Labour Sciences at the Lisbon University Institute (ISCTE – IUL) is one example of a scheme helping bring academic research into corporate life. Finally, the city is building a mammoth, 30,000 m^2 innovation space in a former military food factory. Although plans are still in progress, this should be located in the Beato Marvila district, and be used by small and large companies as a base, for new accelerator and incubator programs and all sorts of cultural events to benefit business life. This year, the city estimates that it has around 400 startups in its incubation and acceleration programs, with more than 1,000 entrepreneurs beginning their journey in Lisbon. More than $140m has been invested in its startups in the last three years, for example, in leading lights such as Uniplaces.

Why should companies come to Lisbon?
We aren't just aiming to be one of the most competitive, creative and innovative cities in Portugal. We need to compete in the international landscape because we are an amazing, global city. We have a lot of assets: we are in a strong geographic, geopolitical position, we are a university city, and we have a lot of creative people, spaces and entrepreneurial skills.
Five years ago, we were in the middle of our major financial and economic crisis, and the city of Lisbon had never been known as a place to invest, study, start up your own company or work. But things have changed because we have really worked on entrepreneurship, investment and knowledge in a very strategic way.

We are not innocents: we are pulling some strings to make Lisbon a dynamic place for new businesses. Startup Lisboa isn't just municipality-owned but we are the leaders. FabLab Lisboa is the most important open-access lab in the country. We are supporting some acceleration programs with investment, acting as leaders in some schemes, partners in others and just doing what we can to further other projects. In this way, we foster a universe of entrepreneurship. When we were named a European Entrepreneurial Region of the Year, this was a massive accolade for Lisbon. It was the first big award related to business that the city had won, since it had previously been recognized for tourism and cultural life.

And when Lisbon won the Web Summit – another massive vote of confidence – its chief executive, Paddy Cosgrave, told the Financial Times our widespread enthusiasm helped persuade him. He said: 'On Twitter I couldn't wake up any morning without somebody saying "hey, you should come to Lisbon; let me know if you'd like to learn more".'

[Contact]   **Iniciativa Lisboa,** Campo Grande 13 B, 1700 - 087 Lisbon
             +351 808 203 232 or +351 218 170 552

[Website]   iniciativa.lisboa@cm-lisboa.pt

Alexandre Nunes Teixeira dos Santos / Sonae Investment Management

Head of Portfolio Development

Sonae IM is Sonae's Corporate Venture Capital, focusing on investing in tech-based companies for the retail and telecommunication verticals. With a flexible investment approach, Sonae IM aims to support businesses in growth stages, always as a strategic partner for their development. Sonae's current portfolio companies are WeDo Technologies, Saphety, Bizdirect, S21SEC, Movvo, InovRetail and Bright Pixel. Sonae IM has 1,050 employees working in offices in twelve countries.

What do you look for in startups that approach you for investment?

All young businesses should do their homework and be able to explain in a straightforward manner what the value proposition of their business is, why they exist, and what they are trying to solve that nobody in the market has already solved. As a startup, you should have a good idea of how unique your solution is (and will be in the future) when compared to other competitive offers in the market. But don't overkill it – some degree of secrecy can work in your favor. If you can show that you have an adequate understanding of the addressable market and competitive landscape, and show numbers and details to prove there is a market for the offering your company is developing, you can gain credibility and show that you have potential and traction in the market. In early stage investments, this is the most important aspect – Sonae IM are essentially investing in the people, not just in the underlying business and technology.Leave no doubt that you have what it takes to make it through with your business. It is crucial that you manage to sell, that you have a great team with the right skill set, a mixture of profiles, dynamics and drive.

Compatibility is essential for a long-term relationship, and that's what you should also seek from an investor. Trust is critical for the good and bad moments you are going to have along the way. Even if the relationship reaches an end at some point, while it lasts, you want it to be a sound and fruitful relationship.

Celso Martinho - Founder and CEO
/ Bright Pixel

Bright Pixel is a group of experienced builders, creative thinkers and investors whose shared goal is to transform two key things: the way companies address innovation and how new ventures are put together.

There are two significant and frequent risks associated with the journey of building a startup – both are critical to the success of any venture. The first is fitting your product or service to the market. Some startups have to pivot their projects way down the road, after months of work, because what they had initially envisioned wasn't quite what their customers needed or wanted. The second is finding your first big customers that will create scale and credibility in the post-MVP phase when you have no track record.

Bright Pixel is positioned to help startups reduce these risks by using its strong ties with industry leaders in the retail, telco and media sectors. Our venture builder studio model consists of a three step lifecycle implementation: it begins in the labs, where we work with larger companies, trying to understand their needs and the reality of their businesses; next is an ambitious incubation program for startups; and finally a seed investment phase. To experiment, showcase and learn from emerging technologies, including those that aren't directly related to our core areas, we know it's key to keep close ties to the universities and local talent. That's why we also organize the largest hackathon and tech cult event in Portugal, Pixels Camp: a community-driven three days of non-stop tech, talks, and workshops, with a forty-eight-hour programming competition, custom-tailored specifically for those who attend the event.

Bright Pixel is Sonae IM's 'company builder studio', focused on early stage investments and startup incubation.

How should a startup approach an investor?

There is no secret recipe, but there are some golden rules that I can give you:

- Cold calls are unlikely to do any good, and take up a lot of your time. You should avoid sending out emails or making phone calls without having the right angle first. Being referred by someone you know and who has a link to the investor you want to approach might be a good way of getting noticed. Ask that person to pitch in for you and to make the first contact.

- Be in the right places to network – attend events where you increase your probability of bumping into the right people. This takes time and effort, and you can't have the luxury of attending everything, but you should make the effort to attend what you can and define a tactic with specific objectives.

- Study carefully before you put the wheels into motion. It helps if you obtain knowledge beforehand about the entities and investors you want to target. There are different types of investors – some might fit with what you want to do, and others could be, in the long run, the reason you fail.

- Seek advice from other founders that have already fundraised, and discuss internally with your co-founders and key people what you are willing to accept regarding conditions from a potential investor.

- Don't react badly to a NO. Use rejection as fuel to keep going and as a learning process to improve your approach. Insist and persist; never give up. You shouldn't cease trying to get a response out of an investor, even if you already suspect it will be a rejection. Use that to keep in touch and to learn the reasons behind the negative answer. A 'no' today might be a 'yes' tomorrow. Continue to give updates to investors that have said no originally and do your best to continue building enthusiasm around your project.

Do & Don't:

Do it for the passion and not just for the sake of money.

Do be paranoid, focused, and concerned with the fine details.

Do surround yourself with the right people, and seek feedback.

Don't rush or take shortcuts. Winning customers that truly like what you are doing doesn't happen overnight.

Don't get locked into anything you can't get out of easily. Hire wisely, and buy only if necessary.

Don't give up too early. If it isn't working, try it in a different way.

"The whole process is a lot like marriage. Until you close the deal, it is a lot like building any other type of relationship, and you shouldn't rush it and jump at the first opportunity."

How can startups improve their chances of receiving another funding round?

- **Timing is everything.** Raising money is a dance that has to be well coordinated. It all depends on what kind of money you are looking for and what kind of achievements you can present at that moment in time. For example, if you are looking for investment to fund your MVP that is still in the oven, you need to show progress.

- **Be confident of what you can deliver with the money you're asking for.** Sometimes it's better to just ask for bridge or convertible loans to avoid valuation discussions that tend to be hard to manage if you're in the middle of your next major milestone.

- **Remember that value is always a relative and subjective notion.** Try to have a detailed rationale that allows you to sustain the inherent value you believe your company is worth. Cash flow is always the best measure of value, but because it might be hard to get in the early stage, focusing instead on customer traction can be an excellent proxy/alternative.

- **Be open to assuming the risk of not reaching the value you believe your company is worth,** e.g., consider models by which you lose a percentage of capital if you do not get a certain customer and/or the revenue expectations in terms of the business plan. Managing expectations is key.

- **Having a clean cap table from the start is crucial.** Don't give up a high percentage of capital in the beginning: preferably no more than 25 percent, and don't allow for too many shareholders, advisors, business angels, family, and fools! It's easier said than done but weird, complex cap tables, in the beginning, can decrease the interest of potential investors going forward. Take special care in analyzing the merits of public funding, as their money often has strings attached that can scare other investors in a future round. And avoid having high valuations too soon in the game, because that can be a real pain and kill your project going forward.

3 steps each startup should take, from idea to scale-up:

- Iterate your idea with your target customers.

- Surround yourself with the right people.

- Trust the people you work with and delegate.

[Contact]   Sonae - Lugar do Espido - Maia
00351 939650502 / ants@sonaeim.com

[Links]   Web: **sonaeim.com** Facebook: **Sonae IM** Twitter: **@sonaeim**

Marcos Soares Ribeiro & Luís Costa / Santander Totta

Head of Santander Universidades Portugal / Head of Marketing

Banco Santander Totta is one of the largest privately owned banks in Portugal, and is part of Santander Group. Since 1988, through both acquisitions and internal growth, the bank now commands a 15 percent market share in this country.

The bank, profitable even during the economic crisis, has a four-pronged strategy to benefit shareholders, clients and employees, while making a clear contribution to society. Its strategy around higher education is part of this social responsibility area, helping to prepare students for future employment and entrepreneurial life. On an international level, the organization has long-term relationships with 1,200 universities, and every four years it invites leaders to a conference to debate current challenges. The most recent was in Rio de Janeiro, Brazil, in 2014, and that discussion set the frame for the individual programs arranged with universities.

The Portuguese universities strategy supports four main schemes. Each year the bank sponsors 200 students to study abroad, mostly in Latin America, and in other higher education institutions that are part of the Santander universities network. Santander Totta gives cash to research programs, and also has a project to match hundreds of students a year with internships through a virtual marketplace, offering them financial support for this period.
Finally, it encourages universities and polytechnics to turn their expertise into entrepreneurship by sponsoring startups competitions, offering free advice and cash prizes of up to €25,000. In the polytechnic sector in Portugal – a third of higher education – the bank sponsors the main startups competition and smaller regional contests. It also links around forty universities in Iberia and Latin America in an association called RedEmprendia, whose initiatives include an international startups contest, with links to potential investors. RedEmprendia has also invested in one winner, a Portuguese company called LaserLeap Technologies. This business avoids injections by using laser technology to permeate the skin, and can be used for cosmetics, skin cancer drugs, vaccines and anesthetics.

Do & Don't:

Do plan your financial needs.

Do get adequate capital, and the right balance of equity capital.

Do take care of your people and support them in gaining skills.

Don't spend too much time on minutiae.

Don't be too cautious about giving away equity and control.

Don't overstretch the idea.

 3 steps each startup should take, from idea to scale-up:

- Understand the true value of the research you are doing and how you could develop it into a business.

- Bring in partners to help – and turn from ideator to a team player.

- Take advantage of tech transfer experts at universities to help create a company.

What should a startup consider when choosing a bank for their company?

MR: Choose a credible bank with innovative solutions. You must choose the right capital structure for your business, and a bank can help you be clear about that: how much equity and how much debt? Don't just think about your banking function, but about how well connected the organization you choose is for your needs. Startups can find more than financial services at Santander, for instance. One of the critical aspects is how your technology relates with other technologies, and we can also help you navigate the university world. If you find complementary researchers to talk to, this can bring new innovations and processes to your project. You should be looking for a banking partner that helps you fund the business, who also has international products and a network that might be helpful for you to sell your goods and services abroad. In our bank we firmly believe human capital is also a key competitive edge in businesses and we have solutions to support our clients in this regard.

When you look at a bank, look at the whole relationship. It's difficult for any one bank to have the best price on every item, so look for a package you are comfortable with. Trust is something a bank can offer, as well as security on all transactions we make.

How do you open a bank account and should you have separate business and private ones?

LC: It's as simple as coming to one of the branches or phoning directly. We can help you immediately. People can bank here in English or Spanish (and of course, Portuguese). We're an international bank and all our internal communications in the group come in three languages. Banks have to make sure their customers understand everything, as part of compliance legislation.

You should have a separate personal account, absolutely detached from your business life. It gives you transparency, focus and clarity about your financial affairs even if you are bootstrapping – funding the business yourself – or not taking a salary. Be absolutely transparent on that, even if you start a business with your money, not least because you have fiscal obligations. You must have separate accounting for your business, even if there are different costs associated with a business bank account. It might be cheaper to have a private account, but does it really make a difference saving on pennies and potentially losing pounds? Your focus should be on thinking and developing the business, and you can rely on your financial partner to discuss your financial options and business-related issues. Researchers are used to working alone in a laboratory, but you need help. A startup is a networking exercise.

"Understand the value of your idea. Then, a good banking partner, the right kind of debt for your business stage and absolute clarity about your accounting will help you focus on growing the business."

What is the difference between an investor and a banker, and when should a company chose one over the other?

MR: It all comes down to risk. If you're at a risky stage of your business, like a startup, you should be looking to have a strong capital structure in terms of equity. When you compare debt to equity ratios, you should have a high level of equity. For a mature company, a bank can structure more sizable financing amounts at a lower cost than equity. A startup should look for a financial partner to give you the right expectations, focus on transaction-related financing, and then as the company matures, you can start taking on debt in a sensible way. When you start generating recurring income, banks can offer sizable amounts. People tend to think, looking at financing, a bank should finance a whole startup business. You should secure a decent equity amount beforehand, and if needed, you should be looking for venture capitalists who are willing to take this kind of risk.

How important is it to be organized about finance?

LC: Your accounts should always show a clear picture of your cash flow predictions, especially at an early stage. Try to get all the instruments from the bank that you need to anticipate as much as you can. Be prepared for cash flow volatility. If you project that you have a need for additional money in a certain period of time, that's a risk, so you should be prepared beforehand with a relevant overdraft or loan.

Of course, some things one cannot predict. You must trust your banking partner to help with that, but the more you can plan ahead for your business, the better. It gives you credibility and that's very positive when you present yourself and your project to your bank. The bank needs to build its relationship with you, but you as an entrepreneur need to show you can be trusted too.

Do startups fail through cash flow issues?

MR: There are so many good reasons for a startup to fail, and lack of cash seems to be a recurrent issue investors and entrepreneurs should be prepared for that and willing to take the risk, and learn from it. But a lack of capital means things weren't planned beforehand with a bank or venture capitalist – and to attract capital, you need a clear business and funding plan. If you have money for one year, at the end of nine months you should assess if the business is viable and if it isn't, close it.

[Contact]   Universities program: **+35 1 21 780 73 24** / apoio4u@santander.pt

[Links]   Web: **santandertotta.pt** Facebook: **santanderuniversidadesportugal** Twitter: **@SantanderUniPL**

Jason Nadal / Microsoft

Lead Evangelist, Microsoft Portugal

How do you catch the cloud and pin it down? And bring blue skies back to your business at the same time? Microsoft is doing just this, reinventing itself as a cloud computing company that holds a shower of other devices and software. The international technology company, founded by Paul Allen and Bill Gates back in 1975, is best known for software products such as Windows and Office – often bought with new computers. PC sales have been in a pattern of steady decline, and Microsoft has had some tougher years. But it is now re-forging itself with a host of different products (including Xbox, Skype, Windows phone and Microsoft Surface tablet) and a new focus on cloud computing – connecting customers via internet to their software solutions and data, held in big data centers. Here, it has had impressive growth, challenging market leader Amazon, according to quarterly earnings reported in July 2016.

Today, more than 1.2 billion people use Microsoft Office in 140 countries around the world, its fibre optic network could stretch to the moon and back three times, 80 percent of companies in the Fortune 500 use the Microsoft Cloud … while 40 percent of cloud platform Azure's revenue comes from startups and independent software vendors. The company won plaudits from the start for providing an innovative, millennial-friendly work environment, and it donates impressive amounts of cash and software to charities and nonprofit organizations. Chief executive Satya Nadella, appointed in 2014, says the mission is 'to empower every person and every organization on the planet to achieve more … harmonizing the needs of both individuals and organizations' in this mobile-first, cloud-first world. And Microsoft is conjuring up an impressive cloud business like a nimble, rain-dancing weatherman.

How does Microsoft engage with startups?
Storyo is an app that makes your pictures tell a story: you choose a time period, and the app turns phone snaps into a tale to share instantly with your friends, complete with maps, music and captions. This Portuguese startup is one of those showcased by Ativar Portugal, Microsoft Portugal's umbrella for work with early-stage companies, governmental agencies, accelerators, venture capitalists and their clients. Each year, Microsoft sponsors and organizes an Ativar Portugal conference to link thirty or more startups with the people they need in order to grow. This brings the startup mentality to Microsoft too, as interesting solutions can do some 'speed-dating' with internal teams to solve customer issues.

Do & Don't:

Do think about the whole: both the business side and the technology side.

Do be iterative. Talk to the community and potential clients to improve your iterations.

Do find a mentor who has been there before.

Don't go to market before you're really ready.

Don't be so hard-coded that you think you're the only one with the knowledge.

Don't focus on just one client.

3 steps each startup should take, from idea to scale-up:

- Prove out your idea: make sure there's a market and seek technology advice.

- Hire outside the box. Everybody has something amazing to offer.

- Understand your needs in the next three to six months.

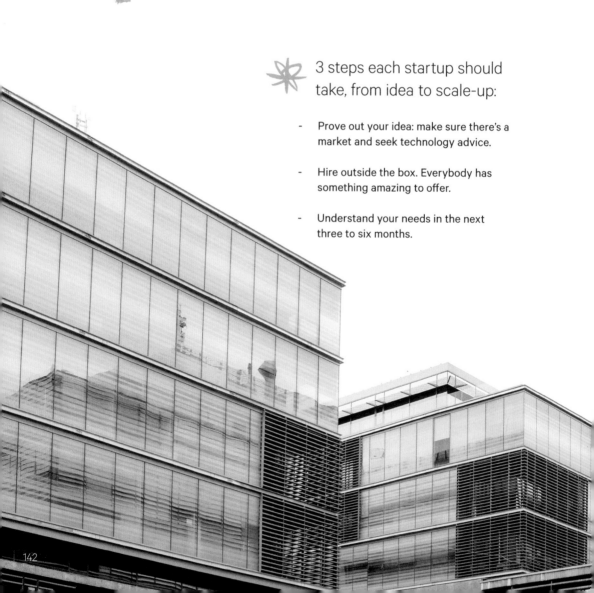

As a global company, Microsoft runs seven accelerators, and Portuguese startups such as the music-streaming/fan base business Tradiio have benefitted from these. A package called BizSpark offers startups three years of free software, services, tech support and access to the Azure cloud to build their products (with any open source language, and keeping their intellectual property). Tripaya, for instance, is a Portuguese startup using Azure, where customers enter their budget and type of holiday they want and the free website comes up with the best deals. Some sponsorship companies come in, flash a bunch of cash and then pull out. Microsoft's job is to be invested in the long-term success of the startup community in Portugal. Sponsors should be evangelizing to its clients and customers about what's next in its technology, but also about companies that are building what's next.

How can connecting with startups help larger organizations like Microsoft?

We have relevancy in the marketplace. The more we are working with startups, mentoring and coaching, the more doors we can open for you from both a product and customer perspective. We know our customer base and can bring in some new, innovative ideas through our startup investments and engagements, helping both our customers and the startups. Clientscape, a Portuguese startup helped by Microsoft, has a way of engaging with your customers by analyzing social media to solve issues faster, with fewer customer service people. One of its clients has solved more customer issues with five people using this cloud-based software than with a customer service team of twenty-five. We look at how we can help them architect their product, allow them to use the cloud in order to scale, help them use the tools they have more effectively and introduce them to more customers with similar needs.
New ways of using technology and looking at problems can give a company like Microsoft potential answers for our customers' problems, whether that's an airline, bank or football club. Working with startups that think they have found a niche to solve things can really open up conversations.

Our job at Microsoft is to provide platforms for companies and customers to develop their own products. The consumer sees Office, Outlook, Windows: those are products we have, but they can also be platforms for people to make their own software solutions. The intelligent cloud – which is what we call our safe, secure cloud platform – is the foundation for allowing all that to happen.

When should a startup seek software expertise?

In building a product, you need to investigate your technology as soon as your idea is crystal-lized – not cemented, because as a startup you need to be open to morphing your product and idea. Running a lean startup is very in vogue. There are so many free tools for developers to

"*Most startups that get past the ideation stage will die of indigestion, not of starvation. They don't know how to handle what they have in front of them. Leads come in and they don't know how to scale in order to meet the demand.* "

build products, including Microsoft, that you need to be very strategic about your architecture to use those tools in the right manner. You can stretch your dollar while still being extremely professional. But if you're using a bunch of free products, you as the leader of the company had better be attuned to when your people stop being efficient with those free tools. That's when you should investigate paying for infrastructure to build products.

Software companies offer free trial periods to develop products, and to know if one – or which one – is right for you, be engaged in your startup community. Reach out to the larger software companies like Microsoft, IBM, Amazon, SAP and understand what startups they are working with. Get out from behind your desk: it's about engagement and asking questions. A lot of startups think they know all they need to know: no, you don't. Microsoft will say if we are not the ones you need to be talking to right now.

How can cloud services help businesses?

There's so much data being collected right now – how do companies make intelligent, real-time decisions with this? How can you get cloud machines making decisions for you based on a parameter, data or information you have given it so that it can start to understand and anticipate your customer needs on its own to provide a better service? How do you communicate with your customer base, in other words, 'conversation as a platform'. The sexy term in the marketplaces is 'bots'. Let's say you go online to Virgin Atlantic and need to talk, you're typing in questions to a platform which uses machine learning and data, and it can start giving the right answers without human involvement. These are some of the exciting things that are happening and approaching quickly. The internet of things will mature. How do you make decisions based on the data from your receivers out there, whether it's on your farm or parking garage or along your oil and gas pipeline? What's the evolution of the internet of things to make better business decisions, whether that's maintenance or investment?

The majority of the cloud is helping businesses with their customers, whether they are consumers or businesses. We're just scratching the surface of the cloud. Is there a nasty rainstorm of security implications behind it? Big companies are wickedly focused on cyber security, which is a threat that isn't going to go away, and there has been a big evolution around protecting your privacy.

[Contact]   thejourney@microsoft.com

[Links]   Web: microsoft.com Twitter: @PTMicrosoft Instagram: microsoft

Maria Luisa Silva
/ SAP Startup Focus

Director, SAP Startup Focus program

SAP stands quite simply for Systems, Applications and Products, and was founded in Germany in 1972. Today, the business software systems company has 320,000 small, medium and large customers in 190 countries and 110 million subscribers to its cloud-based offerings. One of its latest platforms is SAP HANA, which converges database and application platform capabilities in-memory to transform transactions, analytics, predictive and spatial processing so businesses can simplify and operate in real-time. This helps clients use big data analysis to benefit the business – so a retailer could monitor minute-to-minute sales and restock ice creams quicker if the weather were hot, for example.

The Startup Focus program was created in 2012 to enable the company to drive innovation beyond SAP's traditional boundaries. It makes its new platform available not just to current clients but also young companies with bright, innovative ideas that fit well with it, to exploit its potential. The program offers up to $25,000 worth of credits and certifications during a startup's early life, with free use of SAP HANA for product development purposes. It accepts companies mostly focusing on big data, the internet of things, plus predictive and real-time analytics. They can get access to the firm's technical, marketing and sales experts and partners, an introduction to its customers and a chance to pitch to venture capitalists (with no equity or fees taken for program membership). When startups mature in the program they will be exposed to the market and can be offered multiple GTM collaboration options from OEM licensing, to co-sell agreements on a case-by-case basis. Once they become successful, they are more prone for investment and may be acquired as it happened with Multiposting and KXEN. The SAP Startup Focus Program has more than 3,500 early-stage companies building applications on HANA, and has validated more than 230 solutions ready for sale.

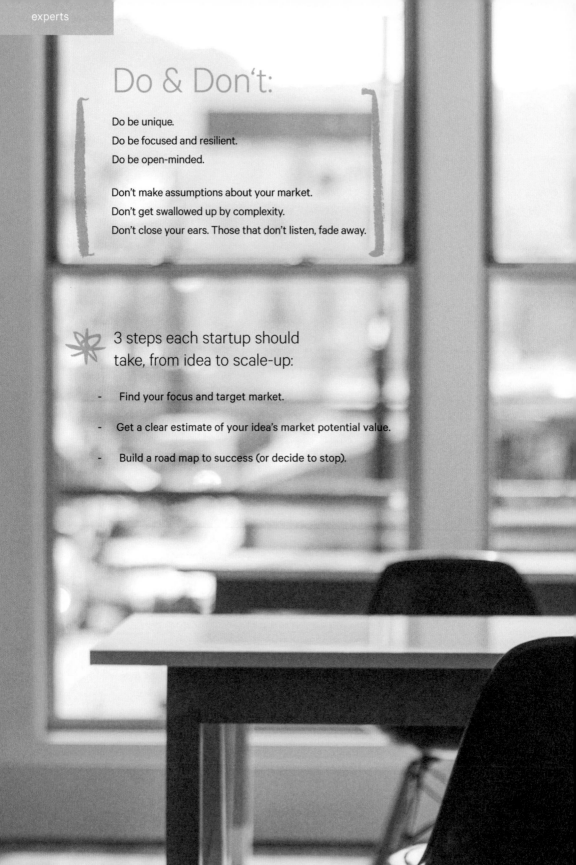

Do & Don't:

Do be unique.
Do be focused and resilient.
Do be open-minded.

Don't make assumptions about your market.
Don't get swallowed up by complexity.
Don't close your ears. Those that don't listen, fade away.

3 steps each startup should take, from idea to scale-up:

- Find your focus and target market.

- Get a clear estimate of your idea's market potential value.

- Build a road map to success (or decide to stop).

Can startups help bigger companies stay on top of technological changes?

Startups can give bigger companies agility, energy and also develop specific expertise. Startups with cloud-based solutions, for instance, can help accelerate the cloud strategy of a bigger company. For SAP, sharing its HANA technology with startups means there are infinitely more possibilities in the same period of time. Millennials are used to swapping houses with Airbnb. This is a similar, modern kind of exchange: the bigger company lends its software, and the startup lends their fresh point of view. Startups don't have clients to attend to, they operate at speed and this barter can change the way the world runs much faster.

Larger firms can also explore new areas minimizing risk. 'Around 60 percent of startups in our program work outside SAP's traditional space,' says Luisa Silva. 'Startups coming from health and research science, for instance'. One alumnus of the program is Meteo Protect, a French company that measures the impact of weather conditions on a business. It was originally pitched to insurance companies but can give many firms a critical competitive advantage. What if there's bad weather in Ghana and you're a chocolate-maker? You could predict cocoa price rises and buy ahead or swap supplier. Semantic Visions, a Czech startup and another example, measures public data in the top ten languages in real time to identify more than 500 different types of threats – which is very valuable for risk management or government intelligence services. Both mean the larger company's technology is employed in new and unexpected fields. Larger companies also need to spend most of their time caring for current customers, rather than focusing on R&D; research and development are all an early-stage startup does.

How can a large company help a startup grow from an idea into a tangible product or service?

Many bigger companies have accelerator programs or work with students at university to help them develop ideas: with access to their technology and expertise, startups' chances of success increase exponentially. SAP, for instance, has two different schemes: University Alliances pick ideas at a very early stage, typically with students. It uses techniques like design thinking to help them go from forming ideas to defining precisely what they want to bring to market. If you come to Startup Focus for acceleration, you should already have an idea of your 'use case'. The program, and others like it, offers technology licenses, technical guidance throughout development and access to training to help your team build up skills.

"Corporates are often complex, but they don't have to be inflexible or dinosaurs. We want to help drive digital transformation through open innovation to our customers, bringing our technology to and through you, the startups. "

After you have a minimum viable product – the most core, testable technology – the business offers access to cloud-based marketplaces and customer exposure at relevant events. This kind of introduction comes easily to a big company, but is invaluable. These kinds of industry programs identify 'high potential startups' for special coaching and mentoring: these, the crème de la crème, will get exposure to top customers. 'It's a win-win-win,' says Luisa Silva. 'The startup gets market access opportunity much faster, and when they position their solution, they are also positioning SAP's technology. And the use case value proposition is a win for the customer.' Meanwhile, if your fresh thinking creates a fantastic little company after this kind of business accelerator, you might find you have a strategic partner or an instant buyer.

What should a startup consider when building a company?

Even though millennials are used to getting things free, true entrepreneurs know that if they build everything from scratch, they will take much longer. If you're in software and want to focus on targeting the market faster, there needs to be a balance between what you build from scratch and what you use that exists, even if it has a cost now or at a future stage. You may need to pay for some things. Startups need to really study the market, what they can bring to it, and listen to feedback. The people who have gone wrong don't listen. They live in a separate world. When someone comes to a potential client and speaks about bits and bytes but hasn't taken the time to perceive what value they can bring to their target market, they have no chance. Why should people buy it? If you don't listen, people won't listen to you either. But when other people's money is in place, startups become much more accountable: venture capitalists and investors will be pushing you to find a good market-fit and start making money.

It's also worth considering the equipment needed to build a company. Although there's free, open source software available for business processes like invoicing, running your supply chain and human resources, you might start feeling the pain when big customers are relying on deliveries. Consider what kind of business infrastructure you need, and think about paying for a professional software.

Luis Manuel & Carla Pimenta / EDP Inovação

Executive Director / Head of Entrepreneurship

EDP is an energy company with activities in production, distribution and sale of electricity and gas. EDP Inovação promotes innovation within the EDP Group. It has a resource and competence base that allows us to support innovative companies regardless of its maturity stage. We have set up a business incubation process, EDP Starter, which leverages on our corporate VC arm, EDP Ventures, and the insights of our business and technology experts. Through EDP Starter we crowdsource ideas from startups from all over the world, allowing us to scout for innovative technologies, solve business challenges and expand into new markets. We take startups working in the energy sector through a structured collaboration process – from the idea stage to venture capital investment.

Every year EDP Starter runs a Seed Race in which the best performing startups become eligible for investment by EDP Ventures. We also help startups to fundraise through our business angels and venture capital network. To contribute to startup success, currently twelve EDP interim managers devote twenty percent of their time to working with startups helping them on specific tasks. We also accelerate payments to startup suppliers (typically less than a month). Feedzai is a good example of our cooperation with startups: one of the first businesses to be incubated by EDP Starter, it deployed its product in our distribution network, in our B2B management system in Portugal, and also in our windfarm remote control system in the US. They received an A round investment from EDP Ventures and other partner VCs. In 2015 its turnover reached €20 million, making it one of the most successful Portuguese startups. We have many success stories and we want to contribute to many more, while improving our business doing it.

How can energy companies aid startups who are still building their business?

Energy is a complex sector where technology and power resource diversity and customer needs are matched instantaneously through an impressive set of special rules and regulations that present significant differences from one country to another. A startup can have a hard time just trying to understand the basics of this complex and demanding environment. Established utilities in the energy sector can act as guides to small companies that want to get in somehow. Knowing the key stakeholders and easily accessing them is halfway to getting your project rolling. Energy startups struggle to find technological partners during the first year and here

Do & Don't:

Do ask for advice before diving into your new energy venture.

Do search for strategic investors.

Do commit to your project, believe in it, and work on it full time.

Don't work alone. Teams will help you succeed.

Don't hide technological information from your potential investors.

Don't give up.

3 steps each startup should take, from idea to scale-up:

- Debate your idea with several industry experts.

- Engage with a technological partner/investor.

- Take some time elaborating your bill of materials.

large utilities can make a huge difference. It's not about having a big checkbook but rather having knowledge, expertise, networking and advantages in procurement, distribution and manufacturing, as well as sales and marketing advantages. The energy sector deals with high scale technology assets that require very tight operation and safety rules, while at the same time it is required to provide power wherever the client needs it at the exact moment when they request it. This leads to the development of a culture of process orientation and cautious decision-making. The forefront of the industry has developed Open Innovation units that can act as startup caretakers and promote the engagement with the operational business units, thus facilitating the establishment of commercial relationships. This is a precious help for startups trying to access large utilities as a core market and we at EDP are proud to be amongst those that support their efforts in this manner. Despite startups being very good at thinking outside the box and creating innovative technologies and irreverent business models, utilities have their own problems to solve. Paying close attention to competitions, awards and specific challenges announced by utilities willing to collaborate with startups will help you in targeting possible new ventures in the energy industry.

How do startups help big energy companies solve specific problems?

While large companies are focused on identifying the problems and barriers, startups are prone to finding solutions and opportunities. Big companies often launch things they can make, not what people really want. Successful energy companies are focused on growth but they are much better at scaling proof of concepts than creating new products from scratch. They have a lot to gain from accessing startups' abilities to create and demonstrate their technologies and business models via early-stage investment. Successful collaboration between startups and energy companies must go beyond financial deals: an enthusiastic and mission-oriented mindset will create better odds of success. Moreover, startups must be multidisciplinary rather than purely technological, innovative or resilient. Scalability and internationalisation paths are basic requirements. Living outside the big "utility box" enables startups to look at the future from totally different angles, pinpoint areas of the value chain that can be completely reoriented through technology convergence, multi-sectorial approach or simple replacement of old fashioned processes by alternatives coming from other industries.

This is something that a large utility cannot do as effectively because of its own nature and mindset. EDP is specifically scouting for startups that can bring added value innovation in five areas of expertise: i) client-focused solutions (innovative products and services and customer satisfaction and engagement); ii) cleaner energy (alternative clean generation and improvement of our power plants efficiency); iii) smarter grids; iv) data leaps (big data, cloud computing, advanced analytics and internet of things); and v) energy storage. We are strong believers of crowdsourcing and we follow an open innovation model which allows us to work together with startups in these fields.

"*Effectively engage with leading energy companies, understand their goals and strategies, share what you are doing, and listen.* "

How might a startup get involved in the energy sector?

In the past, oil and coal were the prime raw materials, now data is taking the lead. In this field a lot can be done and EDP is paying close attention to big data, artificial intelligence, data security and development of people. This is one of the areas where startups can be the most attractive to utilities. Small businesses with a lighter and more flexible structure, which has its genesis in the concept of innovation, can be much faster and more effective at extracting value from the growing flow of utility generated data. To get involved in the energy sector, startups must understand who the key players are, understand their strategy and find support amongst them. A key element in dealing with large utilities is to find the right entry door. The first contact with a conventional unit of a large utility can be rather frustrating for a startup because there's just too much gap between what a startup is looking for and what a utility business unit can give. A clear sign that a utility is opening its doors to startups is when it launches a specific program such as EDP Starter to collaborate with entrepreneurs. They are there to fill in that gap, and that's where entrepreneurs should start. Despite that EDP Starter is still based in three of EDP's geographies (Portugal, Spain and Brazil), both programs run globally, meaning that we accept applications from startups anywhere in the world. These are the main entry doors into the EDP Innovation ecosystem.

What do you think the energy sector will look like in the future?

The energy sector is in the middle of a revolution. Renewable power will continue to grow, but this is no longer done exclusively through large scale wind or solar farms. Centralized power generation will continue to be dominant over the next decades, but the real change is coming from the growth of distribution assets that are connected to the power system. Distributed solar generation, already a reality in many places, will be one of the fastest growing segments in energy production; a very significant share of consumers will have generation capacity at their homes. Some of them will own those assets but, most likely, the majority of them will simply allow for the power supplier to install them in order to improve the competitiveness of the supply. Electrification of the economies will increase, driven mostly by an increased electrification of transport through electric vehicles. They will not only contribute to a much better environment in our cities but can also play an important role on grid stabilization once their battery storage capacity is used, not only to acquire power from the grid but also to sell it to the grid. Storage may also be provided locally through the installation of batteries at customers houses. This will contribute to match to local production to the local consumption and minimizing the need to import and export from the grid. With PV panels, storage and EVs, the customer will need to have a local Home Energy Management tool that makes sure that they get all the power they need, whenever they need it, and at the lower possible cost.

[Contact]   Av. 24 de Julho, 12 - 1249-300 Lisbon Portugal
+351 21 001 89 03 / edpstarter@edp.pt

[Links]   Web: edpopeninnovation.edp.pt Facebook: edpopeninnovation Twitter: @edp_open

views

Filipa Neto

Co-Founder and Managing Director / Chic by Choice

Filipa Neto has spent €1,000 on a dress before. Now that her online dress rental business
Chic by Choice is showing it has legs, she'd expect to be buying quite a few nice frocks.
The twenty-five-year-old smiles and steps into a dress wardrobe that not many wealthy women
own – all colours, lengths and a flourish of styles from Alice by Temperley to Valentino, lining
the walls of a whole room in her Lisbon office suite. 'Now, I just rent them,' she says.

This is Chic by Choice today. But how did it all start?
There are two co-founders, me and Lara Vidreiro. I was studying economics, Lara was studying
business and we were in the same class at CATÓLICA-LISBON university. We had this gala
coming up and although we loved fashion, we started thinking we would not ask for a lot of
money from our parents again for a new dress as we were in a really deep crisis in Portugal.
Lara started saying: what if you could wear something and return it, and it was legal?!

Because students might do that sneakily anyway?
Yes. What if there were this physical store where you could go, wear it for the night and return
it? To wear it, return and only pay a fraction of the price because we were not going to wear it
ten times. I said, what if it were online and you could have all these amazing, exclusive brands
from abroad? It was 2011, and that year we saw a poster of an incubation competition, called
'Realize o Seu Sonho' – make your dreams come true – from Acredita Portugal. It was a three
month process, you had challenges, and we were doing the business plan, testing, doing
surveys. Of 3,000 ideas, we got second place. The prize was services, lawyers, press coverage
and recognition. We decided to give ourselves six months, and if we raised money, we would
start a company.

And did you?
We got our first investment and long story short, it was a lot of money and not the right partner
or deal. It was a business angel, we didn't have the majority of the company, Style in a Box, we
were not the directors. But we were starting in an era where there was no benchmark. Our first
big mistake was trying to launch too fast, without the right organizational structure. We also
started testing in Portugal and Spain, which weren't good e-commerce markets.

What should you have done instead?
You have to go to the market where you think your chances are higher. Our vision was that
we needed to move the business to the UK. In the long term, there would always be situations
like this where we would need to negotiate on things that to us were obvious and relied on the
speed of execution. So we realized the best thing was to negotiate to leave the company, which
we did.

In 2014, you started Chic by Choice…
I moved to London for the first year and a half, spending most of my time there. We started to raise money again. We developed and tested a lot of ideas around the stock model.

What stock did you think you'd need?
When we started Chic by Choice, everything was according to demand. A retailer would allow us to use their photos on our website, and if there was demand, we would buy into the brand at the wholesale price.

And today?
Today we have orders so fast that we would lose money if we waited for demand. Right now, a dress gets uploaded and two days later it's rented. So shipping from the US, where we have most of our partners, to Lisbon then the UK where we have most of our customers would take more than these two days.

How much money did you raise?
Pre-seed round, we started with €500,000. We tested for around eight months, finding out demand and then started working with a buyer.

How much is art and how much is data knowing what people want to rent?
It's mostly data and then for the art, what we call the window pieces, I would say it's around 10 percent. People have the tendency to like the same.

What do they like?
Our customer is a woman between twenty-five and forty-five years old, who wants to look sophisticated. A lot of the events are corporate events, so most of them choose a round neckline to feel comfortable. Colours are associated with being classy or powerful, like black, red, classic colours. They also love lace. If you look at the website, everything looks different but in terms of attributes, they are really similar. We have more than 1,300 dresses online, 70 percent are rented in the UK, 15 percent in Germany and then it's the rest of Europe.

Who are your customers?
Most of them work in marketing, law, consultancy, and they are already at a stage in their career where they are invited to work events that aren't just meetings. Even in cool startups, people at C-levels are renting dresses. It's quite exciting to see that! Don't tell them…

What does it cost?
The starting price is £50, but you always get a discount on the first rental of £25. Prices can go up to €200, and the customer is spending, on average, €100. The rent is 15 percent of the consumer price.

What are your most popular brands?
There's Badgley Mischka, a timeless US brand, but we also test designers without a lot of distribution in Europe. The number one reason people rent is not because it's more affordable; they want to access something exclusive and don't need it for a long time. It's also about the convenience, since the customer receives two sizes of the same style at no extra cost.

Don't be afraid to fail. Always ask for advice, but in the end follow your own instincts.

Filipa Neto

So, take me back, you went to London for 18 months?

The team was here, and I spent 70 percent of my time there. We went to the UK because we were going to find the formula in a big market. In Portugal, online sales are 0.5 percent, but in the UK it's 14 percent. The population is different, the average amount people spend online per year is ten times more, the numbers made sense.

What surprised you?

The willingness to spend. People spend money in a completely different way, especially if things are exclusive and considered special.

Because people are richer?

Yes, that also helps. For a business like this to work, you have to have events. You have customers who go to the website 100 times, the dresses might be the prettiest things, but they never rent because they don't have events. In London, there's always a reason to go out. Portugal has a more informal culture.

Then you raised €1.5m in investment. Do you and Lara have the majority of equity?

More important than the percentage is are you able to manage the company? If you want to go to those high revenue numbers, eventually you will lose the majority.

How many people do you have?

We have fifteen people full time, and some freelancers on areas like search engine optimisation and UX. It's not easy in Portugal to find good managers, so we recruited our CTO from Berlin: the mindset is a bit different because the startup ecosystem is more mature.

How many men do you employ?

Four men and eleven women. Guess what? The men are all developers. I never felt we were building an unbalanced team because in the tech area there are men involved.

What has gone right (and wrong) in Chic by Choice?

We were really disciplined with building the idea for the UK, and not creating something for us. The first months of business can feel negative as you want them to be amazing. Most likely they will not be. You just need to cope with that anxiety. That discipline helped, managing expectations for yourself, your investors, people who work with you. Most people don't understand companies aren't built overnight. We've had occupancy rates of our summer collection of 80 percent, 90 percent, so now managing the operation has become tricky. In the last six months, I've spent most of my time in Portugal, understanding consumers, informing investors, making sure Chic by Choice is in the ecosystem of startups, the customer knows about it, and recruiting people.

What are the challenges?

We have days where we've shipped sixty boxes in one day. It's not just shipping the product. We need to dry clean it and repair it. What makes us have a better margin than a pure retailer is the fact that the product goes around, but that's also one of the biggest headaches.

Do some things need a lot of repair?
We only have certain dresses that we know are able to perform well in turnaround, but to know this you have to test. The turnaround of the dresses is one of the most important aspects of the business.

You mean the number of times they can be worn?
Or cleaned, and look new. You need the fulfilment of opening a box and it looks like new, right? That's what the customer expects. Depending on the fabric, it can go more than twenty times. We have dresses that have lasted more than 30 times. The buyer process is not just art: it's actually a lot of metrics.

Why are you based in Lisbon?
In Portugal, you have a lot of developers, people who talk a lot of languages for customer service, and people with a lot of market knowledge, and not at a high price. If you were building the same team in London, it would probably cost four times more.

Will you stay in Portugal?
We built this business having most of the team in Lisbon and part in London, and we will continue to do that. At the same time, for logistic purposes, we need to move the warehouse as we ship most orders internationally and in terms of potential revenue from same-day and weekend delivery, and swaps, it makes a lot of sense.

What advice would you give other startups?
Don't be afraid to fail. Always ask for advice, but in the end follow your own instincts. It's really hard to predict the future and it's not a VC, all the past stories, that can predict the future. If Airbnb had sought investment or advice from the hotel industry, there would never have been Airbnb.

Is it a flaw to base your business on someone else's risk?
Yes, but in certain sectors it's almost impossible to build a business without VC money because you need scale. There are only a few stories in e-commerce that have bootstrapped and usually it's brands, not platforms. If you have a brand, you have a big profit margin, but when you have partners, the margins are tighter, so it needs more volume to make the business work.

And how about your team? What culture are you creating?
A culture where people feel happy and empowered, everyone knows the main metrics of the company and everyone is deeply involved.

[About]   Chic by Choice is a designer dress rental website, shipping its selection of more than 1,000 gowns to more than fifteen European locations, including the UK, Germany, France and Italy. It stocks more than forty designers, including leading Asian and American names.

[Links]   Web: chic-by-choice.com Facebook: chicbychoiceworld Twitter: chicbychoicecom

What are you reading?
*The Viral Startup: A Guide to
Designing Viral Loops* by Andrew Chen.

What are you listening to?
Erykah Badu playlist.

What's your favorite app?
Instagram.

What's your favorite podcast?
I don't listen to podcasts.

What are your work essentials?
Cell phone.

What skill do you wish you had?
Programming.

What time do you wake up in the morning?
Most days at 8.00 am.

Nuno Sebastião

Chairman & CEO / Feedzai

On the fifth attempt at interviewing thirty-seven-year-old Nuno Sebastiao, we finally meet via Skype. It's not surprising this charming former aerospace engineer is hard to reach: he spends his time on international flights, sleeps for five hours a night and typically gets up to work between 3am and 5am wherever he is. This focus means that, in five years, he and two co-founders have built a fraud detection startup that might just dominate the world.

Hurray! We meet finally. You're a busy man.
You have no idea. Last week I crossed the Atlantic four times. I was in Lisbon, flew to New York, then Paris, Washington, then Friday night from Washington back to Lisbon.

How many air miles have you got?
I live in San Francisco with my family and took the four of us, my mum and niece to Hawaii just on miles. I always fly with United Airlines and renewed my status in May. It's not a nice thing – but everyone I know in companies that have operations all over the place does that.

Where are your operations?
Feedzai has 125 people, and we expect by the end of the year to have close to 200. Development and operations are in Portugal, delivery, sales and marketing are in the US, the European sales team is headed out of London, and we're hiring for Paris and Frankfurt.

How would you describe Feedzai?
We keep payments across the ecosystem safe. Imagine you're a bank that issues credit cards to consumers. We help the bank understand if it's really them. We help merchants understand if they are on the receiving end of fraud, or shipping goods to the people who bought them. We also track how much fraud we detect and at what cost to annoyed good customers. If you go to another country and your card is declined, it's painful. That's called a false positive: the system picked up something, but it's you! It's important to detect fraud but avoid this friction as well.

Take me back to the beginning – how did you decide combatting payment fraud would make millions and take you to Hawaii?

It took a long time to get there. There's three founders, myself, Paulo [Marques] and Pedro [Bizarro]. Pedro was my first boss in 1999 when I was twenty, a teaching assistant at the University of Coimbra in Portugal who hired me as an undergrad to do some database work for him. We're all computer science guys. I graduated and moved to Germany to work at the European Space Agency – curiously, with Ricardo Marvão from Beta-i. My first company, Evolve Space Solutions, I built with Ricardo, and sold to Novabase in Portugal. Paulo, who I knew from university, had spent a sabbatical year with me doing computer science research at the space agency. From being exposed to computer skills from all over Europe, I knew Paulo and Pedro were second to none. Of the three, I'm the stupid one from a computer science point of view.

But you have the best legs?

I don't know! But all they want to do is build product and aren't interested in sales or company-building. In 2009, I did my MBA in London, while I had the company with Ricardo. I knew I wanted to build something really technical and invited Paulo and Pedro for a weekend in London. We knew nothing about a problem but started from what we were good at: at the European Space Agency, I was running the simulation infrastructure. Pedro did his PhD on how to measure what's happening with auxiliary information – for example, if you measure the temperature right now, what does it tell you if you don't know if it's summer or winter? Paulo worked on building large-scale, distributed systems. We had no idea what to do with this.

But in 2011 you built some technology combining your strengths?

Yes, we had this technology, and thought it could be applied to a number of problems but had no idea where the money was. We tried utilities in 2012 and the Portuguese company EDP gave us €600,000 in seed money to apply it to real-time processing in smart grids, when you'd generate energy at your home and feed it back to the networks. We tried telecoms, monitoring how the network was behaving in order to change load from one cell to another. Then at the end of 2012, a pivotal moment, we met SAP's ventures firm, Sapphire Ventures. They liked what we stood for, thought the engineering was strong but that we had no idea what we were doing from a business standpoint. They were probably right. They gave us some money, not much, $2m.

I wouldn't mind an investment of $2m…

Not for me, for the company! It was good money. They said I should move to the US, and out of three areas, telecoms, utilities and fintech, pick one. We had tiny contracts in all of them so it was hard. We didn't want to get rid of any money, but decided to focus on financial services.

Why?

The biggest contract in December 2012 was with a Portuguese bank, and we could see e-commerce taking off. Millennials were doing all their banking online and you needed to know if that person sitting at the computer was who he or she claimed to be. We could simulate model behavior, measure what was happening in real time, contextualize and do it at scale. Smart grids were too slow for a startup and the programs kind of stalled as EU money dried up. The telecoms service was focused on specific needs, not creating a product that was scalable. So I moved to the US in April 2013 and started talking with all of the banks.

"*We've been well paid as founders and don't do this for money.*"

Nuno Sebastião

How did that go?

2013 was really, really hard. You had a company with no track record in financial services from a country under IMF bailout trying to tell you that they can stop fraud! I sold $20,000 in the US, in a full year.

How were you surviving?

Out of those $2m we raised, we spent more than half. We had money still coming from some of the contracts we had in Portugal but it was peanuts – $2m from services. If in 2014 things had not changed, we would have been out of business by September. But those $20,000 were the best thing we did because they were from Capital One, probably the most technologically advanced bank. They can talk technology at the same level as an SVP at Google or Facebook. When they signed a pilot with us, they were looking for a solution for online account opening. The pilot results were good and in mid-2014 we signed a multimillion dollar contract with them. That's when the company changed: we demonstrated the technology was solid and we could sell it to very large organizations in the United States.

And how was your name, Feedzai, going down?

Engineers suck at naming! But what matters is what you make with it. The most powerful company is the world is called Apple – that's not a good name! It's an apple! Feedzai comes from what we do – processing data feeds – and zai is from the Japanese 'banzai' where people run very fast. It's data feeds, really fast – that geeky. In the beginning, people said: 'What a funky name!' but now it's stronger than the name itself.

So, 2014, you won the multimillion dollar contract. What next?

Sometimes when it happens, it happens all in one go. In the same month, we signed a very large deal with the world's largest processor, First Data, which processes 35 percent of worldwide payment volume. That was game-changing for Feedzai: we were at the table and no-one could say we weren't credible. I stopped every other contract, and shipped all twenty of us to the US. At the end of the year, we won a major contract in India working on fraud detection for SMS-based payment. We were profitable but needed to raise serious money. We could choose, and in April 2015 raised $17.5m from a New York firm called Oak HC/FT that only does fintech. Sometimes when you read too much TechCrunch [online tech news], you want to go for the 'brand' VC, but what matters is the guy who is going to work with you. Sometimes the big VCs lack knowledge, and I'll always work with someone who can help me and knows the space.

And since then?

Since, it has been how much we can sell, how fast we can ramp up, scaling internal processes and people... while making sure we don't screw up the clients we have already won. I hired the guy responsible for Amazon's fraud systems, one of the most well-respected executives in the space. In Europe, I hired Richard Harris, who was running international sales for Experian. And Capital One came in as an investor.

How are you doing financially?

We work with our clients with typically three to five year engagement contracts – the longest is ten years. Last year we finished with a total contract value of $55m, and this year we expect to have $120m, spread over multiple years. Last year, our sales were $19.6m, and this year we expect to end between $35m and $40m.

What lessons have you learned?

A ton. There were days you think it's not going to work, days when people screw you. We had a head of sales who moved to work for a client, which sucks. I was afraid they'd hire all my people and empty the company! They tried, and that would have killed us, but luckily in Portugal people are very loyal. In the US, I've had to fire people on the spot, had people that stole from the company, someone I hired in sales submitted a dinner with clients with $350 bottles of wine, expecting me to pay. Are you crazy? I've never had a $350 bottle of wine. The person said I had no guideline against it, so we had to pay for it but in the US, beautifully, we have employment at will and fired the person the next day. [To build our internal processes] I hired a chief of staff, Kathryn Montilla.

What about your personal life? Have there been sacrifices?

I have twins, born on a Sunday in 2007. My wife was knocked out, I did a presentation on the Monday and went back to the hospital. I deeply believe if you have partners who help, and you're ok with balancing being at home with doing your work, it can be done. We have people everywhere, so if you're responsible and work your ass off, that gives you all the flexibility in the world. I can be two weeks flying and one week at home, not even going to the office but working whatever times I have to work. We've been well paid as founders and don't do this for money. Our investment contract says if we perform according to plan, they cannot force us to sell the company. The three of us really like what we do, have never had so much fun, and only now it's easier. I like it.

How much equity do you still have?

We have less than 50 percent and I'm very critical of this in Portugal. When we raised that seed round in 2011, we gave away almost half of the company. That's wrong. In subsequent rounds, we say that shouldn't have happened, and today we control around 37 percent of the company. One thing we've done well is that we have a controlling function on the board and with voting rights, similar to the guys at Google and Facebook.

What are your aims now?

To really do good for customers. Feedzai will work as a business; doubling the sales will happen. It would also fill me with joy if our early employees had their own companies and I invested in them, as happened with PayPal. My dream, when I grow up, is that Feedzai is a playground for a lot of good people to build their reputation and go on to build other companies. Money, returns, IPO, all of that is secondary.

[About]   Feedzai is a platform to fight fraud and business risk, pairing machine learning with human insight to analyze masses of data in microseconds. It helps banks, merchants and marketplaces accept or reject payments, open accounts, and maintain trust between buyers and sellers – spotting fraudulent activity but avoiding 'false positives' that annoy good customers.

[Links]   Web: feedzai.com Facebook: Feedzai Twitter: @feedzai Instagram: feedzai

What are you listening to?
Bob Marley and reggae.

What's your favorite app?
Prisma

What's your favourite podcast?
Let's Talk Payments.

What are your work essentials?
Headphones, phone, Mac ... and charger! I forgot
one and had to spend a few days without
using my Mac.

What skill do you wish you had?
To be good with my hands, at drawing,
woodwork and metalwork. I'm horribly bad.

What time do you wake up in the morning?
I'm always on different time zones so I sleep
for a few hours, get up, do some work from
3am to 5am, then sleep another hour,
waking at six. I'm wired for about five hours of sleep.

Miguel Santo Amaro

Co-Founder / Uniplaces

Halfway through a conversation with Uniplaces co-founder Miguel Santo Amaro, his watch stops. Appropriately enough, this twenty-seven-year-old from Porto is in a race against time to grab the international market in brokering housing (and more) for students. Today, his business has 150 employees and operations in thirty-nine cities. But it's a long way from the early days, cleaning iffy toilets before photographing apartments to post on Uniplaces.com, in the hope that students would book a year's rental without a single visit.

How did Uniplaces start?

With three co-founders: Mariano Kostelec, the Slovenian/Argentinian; Ben Grech, the British guy; and myself, the Portuguese. The common background was studying in the UK. In 2011, we were discussing future plans; Ben and Mariano wanted to leave their current jobs and I was just graduating from my master's degree, and we decided to try something out.

What attracted you to a student accommodation business?

The end of 2011/2012 was an interesting time for online marketplaces. HomeAway, a listings portal, had just IPO'd at $2bn. Airbnb came in with this transactional marketplace [managing the payment process] and took over. We thought: where can we replicate a similar model? There are 165 million students in the world, no global brand to sort everything out, relocation is a painful experience, and most transactional platforms are for short-term rentals. No-one was doing something proper for students. Universities were a clear marketing channel; students are early adopters of high-tech stuff, and often their experiences had been terrible.

Was this driven by personal experience?

Mariano and I struggled to find accommodation in the UK. Mariano paid twelve months of rent upfront without a guarantor, I had to pay six months of rent in a really expensive residence in my second year, and even Ben from London didn't know exactly where to stay in Nottingham, and viewings were a nightmare. You had to view ten properties, and if it's raining in London, it's even worse.

What happened next?

We spent a couple of months in 2011 brainstorming. The three of us looked at the UK, but didn't want to go there as it was expensive and the lifestyle – especially the rainy weather – wasn't appealing. We ended up looking to Portugal, stayed three months in a family place, then in 2012 we moved to Lisbon's first tech incubator, Startup Lisboa, and spent eighteen months there. In summer 2012, we raised €200,000 from Portuguese and British angels, who connected us with the second round of €800,000 a year later.

How did Uniplaces look in the beginning?

We started with a classified model [listings for a set fee]. We didn't know if students would actually book online, versus just trying to meet the landlord, but in 2013, we went all in and did a transactional marketplace model: students started paying online and we took a commission. That was great. In 2014, we did our seed and post-seed round with Octopus Investments, and raised €700,000 plus £2.2m and expanded internationally. We launched first in Portugal, then the UK. In 2015, we expanded to thirty-nine cities in the major markets in Europe, and raised $24m. We grew the team to 150 today, and have the biggest office of 120 in Lisbon with twenty nationalities. In 2016, we started developing local presence with offices in Spain, Italy and Germany.

What was this all like on the ground?

People have this romanticized view about entrepreneurship where it's all rosy. The first thousand accounts were on-boarded by me and Mariano. That means we had to go clean apartments and toilets to take ok photos for people to book online. We've also had a team of six or seven employees, and had to say: the investors haven't confirmed they are going to give us cash, so there's a big chance that in two weeks we're all out on the streets. Firing some of your best friends wasn't easy – the company changed and needed someone different. Those things are hard to accept and deal with.

What have the business challenges been?

User behavior – really believing that a student would book a house for six months without viewing it, and pay it online, committing €1,000. Also, not having a powerful brand, how could we avoid a perception of being dodgy-looking?
We thought in the beginning we should be in every country in the world, but then we had to centralize to city by city. Then we scaled again to kind of win Europe. It was almost like putting the flag in each market and growing really rapidly. Then understanding again that maybe we should focus, turning every city profitable and only then scaling. You see a lot of startups just scaling prematurely. That was a good lesson. Today we know: let's get the model right, do it really well in six core cities, and then once we hit interesting numbers, scale geographically.

What was wrong with how you had expanded?

It was ad hoc, pressured by competitors, pressured by investment rounds and maybe not as strategic as it should have been.

"We have clear and different strengths and weaknesses, and the business would probably not have worked without one of us. "

Miguel Santo Amaro

Should you have got investment slower?

No, but we should have told the story in a different way. Instead of getting big with extra revenue, what about focusing and really nailing the core activity of the company? That's really hard.

What has shocked you the most?

How many student landlords there are. In Lisbon, our biggest landlord has 350 rooms. The biggest private student landlord in London has 44,000 beds, and there are a lot of clients in that range. I was surprised how students are really sneaky about paying anything and also how people behave in terms of customer service: they complain about everything, make up stories.

Tell me about the business model today. Your website is pitched at students, but how much do landlords pay you?

It's usually something less than 10 percent of the total contract value. We try to be competitive and undercut real estate agents. It also depends on the portfolio size, and the relationship with the landlord, but I'd say between 5 percent and 10 percent. The lesson that we got is that if you want to win any marketplace, you need to focus on supply. If you have all the houses in Lisbon on the platform, whatever happens, students will come to you because you're the only platform. So that's the important thing for us.

But in future you'll aim at the whole student experience?

Students spend $500bn every year on stuff, a third of that on housing. The rest is food, clothing, travel, transportation, Telcos, bills – but there's no brand, company or service that caters for the whole experience. What we think Uniplaces can become is a place where you'll book, discover and live the best university experience you'll ever have. We want to build a network of student ambassadors, we've just created the first crowdsourced scholarship for housing, and want to become the global gateway for the student community: a brand students connect with, and a gateway for other companies and services to tap into. We could do airport pickup services, SIM cards, banks and really cater for communities in specific cities.

So where will most revenue come from?

It will depend on the market, and maturity of the city. I would say the landlords would be willing to pay more if we have their house always full.

Tell me about your competitors.

Real estate agents, not loved by a lot of people, especially students, because of the high fees. Also agencies don't love students. They don't pay that much, and there's a lot of hassle. Foxtons in the UK are a competitor. People sometimes forget the highest renters in London today are international students, more than investment bankers. Other competitors are free channels like Facebook groups, but there's no clear winner in the market yet, no Booking.com, so there's an opportunity.

How profitable is the business?

We are focusing on getting our six core cities into profitability. We are profitable in some, and pushing the net margins. This was the first week when we generated over €1m to our landlords, the total sum of all contracts this week.

Tell me about co-founder dynamics.

We actually didn't know each other that well until we decided to work together, but blended really well. We have clear and different strengths and weaknesses, and the business would probably not have worked without one of us. We know what type of company we want to build: open, hard-working, and we really push for people with low egos, because I think a team always wins.

What's your typical day?

We're hiring two or three people a week, so a lot of interviews. Then one-on-ones with key members of staff, investors and advisors. A Skype call with the other two founders, as we're splitting ourselves between countries. I do sports at the gym in the morning, from 7.30am to 9am. 9am, in the office, usually leave around 8pm or 9pm.

How important is an obsessive focus?

You have to be here with the team, really close to it. As you scale, you become more process-oriented, more organized, and have more resources, so I don't think things should go too crazy. But I think whatever you have to do in life, there's a minimum commitment to have a chance to be successful.

What is success for you?

This business is about maximizing shareholder wealth. The co-founders still have control, which for us is key, and a stake in the company to make us committed to stay there long-term. My personal Miguel Amaro way is to build a successful, global tech company from Portugal. Jack Welch says for you to succeed, you have to get better people than you to do the work. Your job is to inspire, mentor and be part of the journey. I don't think people have to be chief executives for a company's life. And sometimes you have to be really lucky as well.

Do you have any advice for other startups?

Go for a great incubator like Startup Lisboa, which connects you with a whole ecosystem. Enjoy the lifestyle, meet other entrepreneurs around town – interesting people like Anthony Douglas from Hole19, Jaime Jorge from Codacy, the investor Hugo Pereira from Shilling Capital Partners, João Vasconcelos, secretary of state for industry. Look at the whole country too – Braga and Porto.

[About]   Global student accommodation platform, Uniplaces, has been described as the Airbnb of student flats. It takes 5–10 percent of the contract value from landlords, brokering rooms for up to twelve months. Students view and pay their deposit online.

[Links]   Web: uniplaces.com Facebook: Uniplaces Twitter: @Uniplaces Instagram: uniplaces

What are you reading?
Scaling Up by Verne Harnish, and *The Hard
Thing About Hard Things* by Ben Horowitz.

What are you listening to?
Bossa nova from Brazil, Chico Buarque, Caetano Veloso.

What's your favorite app?
I use Uber a lot, and I'm intrigued by Pokémon GO.

What's your favorite podcast?
The Tim Ferriss Show.

What are your work essentials?
Laptop, phone and internet.

What skill do you wish you had?
The ability to stop time.

What time do you wake up in the morning?
7.20am.

Vasco Pedro

Co-Founder and CEO / Unbabel

Vasco Pedro, the thirty-nine-year-old chief executive and co-founder of Unbabel, talks (at 140 words-a-minute) about a company that aims to be 'the world's translation layer', speedily translating content with computer software and human translators.

How do I pronounce 'Unbabel'? Like the tower of Babel, or like a babel – or babble – of voices?
You can say it any way – it works. In America you say babel, about talking. When it comes to languages online, the world is diverging, so there's a parallel with the tower of Babel.

Where did your interest in language and computers begin?
My fascination was always the human mind. I have been coding since I was six, and computers were a great testing ground for how things work. I did a PhD in Natural Language Processing at Carnegie Mellon University in Pittsburgh. This was everything to do with processing language, from the kind of search that Google does to speech recognition and translation. You and I communicate as we have the assumption we understand the world in similar ways. When you cross domains and try to match things up, you have a lot of issues.

What languages do you speak?
Binary! Portuguese, English, Spanish, Italian I understand, I would survive in French, I would not starve in Greek and I took a semester of Japanese, but all I remember now is to say hello.

What was your first company?
It was more like a project of four PhD students, inspired by Professor Luis von Ahn, who said in a lecture: 'game plus dating equals money.' It was about short messages and you could upvote things you had a connection with. Every time you upvoted something, you got a piece of the person who wrote that and if you completed the photo, you got the connection. It was a cute idea but none of us were truly fascinated about that problem. We started getting some traction and thought we would incorporate and build a company around it but we never got to that point, mostly because I went to Google to do an internship.

What was it like at Google?
During that summer at Google, in 2007, Google was la-la land for developers. You went in and said, pick a problem and as long as it's big enough, you had infinite stuff available. There was a restaurant that only served food from Medieval Europe. You needed a bike, you went down to the basement and a guy said: take a bike. It was very well paid: $8,000 a month. I realized Google felt like university, brilliant people around you, but the probability of having a strong impact was very low. I felt, 'I need to do a startup'.

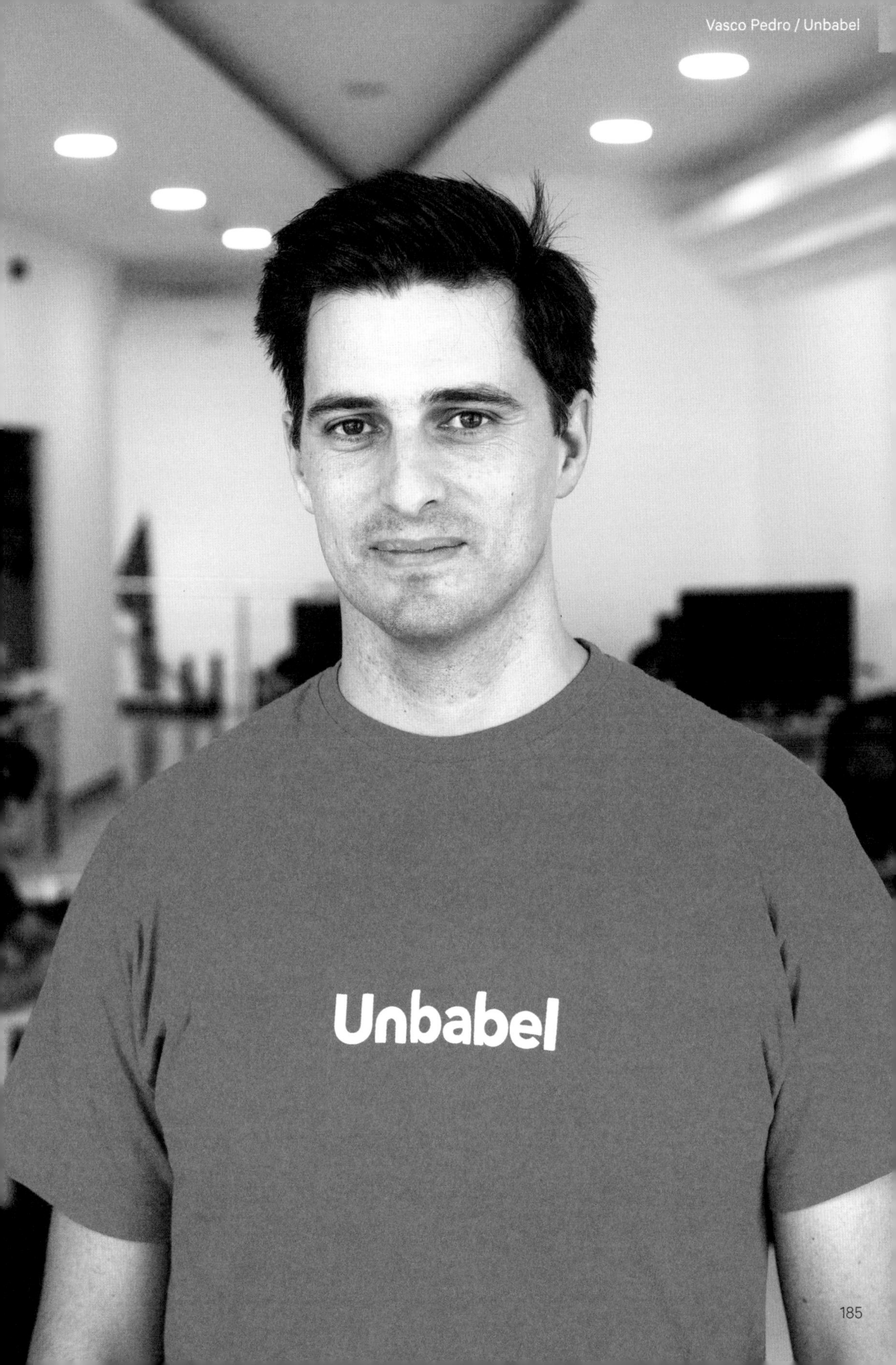
Unbabel

So you started a company?

The first startup was called Bueda, Portuguese for really good. It was about semantic parsing. The idea was, if you had images or video and you had to understand what they were about so you could serve better ads, could you use the tags [the keywords people add when uploading videos] around them? Lesson: starting a company by yourself is really hard.

Because you can't argue with yourself?

That, but also you have a lot of doubts, and they just pile up. Another problem is we had a technology looking for a product and not a problem we were trying to solve. We launched a social media marketing tool and didn't really care about social media marketing so it became, let's not do that.

That company merged into FlashGroup, you left, and returned to Portugal. Why?

I had been thinking about going back to Portugal for a while: two years in the US had turned to ten and three kids. I love the US but I have the feeling I barely escaped! FlashGroup didn't have a CEO. There was no clear, strong vision of how to go to market.

What then?

I joined a startup called Dezine, with this idea of revolutionising the world of fashion, being its app store. The bad idea there was that I knew nothing about fashion! I hired Bruno Silva and Hugo Silva and we realized we really liked working together and were a complementary team.

They became your cofounders at Unbabel, with João Graça. How did the firm come about?

A lot of people asked me to translate stuff, I'd go to Google Translate and correct the translation: I thought, can we do that on a massive scale? We don't know how our brain works so there's a quantum leap that still needs to happen, and we don't believe machine translation's going to solve it in the next five to ten years.

Tell me about building the team of five founders.

We felt our team was amazing but we needed someone to bring in business experience, and Sofia [Pessanha] and I have known each other for years but the timing was never right until Unbabel came along in 2013.

So do your human translators run things through Google Translate and make it right?

We take text, run it through our own machine translator, split it into small chunks and each chunk goes to several people in sequence, the translator corrects it, and somebody else gets and corrects that output. You have this chain until you get to the point where it's perfect.

Is there ever a perfect translation?

That's another reason why we think machine learning isn't going to get there any time soon. If I give you and five people a picture of a cat, it's most likely they are going to recognise that that's a cat. But with a translation, there's no ground truth of the right translation. If you give the same text to five different people, they can all produce valid, different translations.

Startups can have technical debt, doing things fast that you will have to correct. But you can't accumulate emotional debt with co-founders.

Vasco Pedro

But artificial intelligence speeds up the process?

Not just that. It gets the best possible starting text, through translation memories and automatic post editing. You see the original text, as a translator. We have 40,000 people registered with Unbabel as translators. Of those, 6,500 are paid. If I give you a topic you're familiar with, you'll be better, faster and happier. We did a lot of tests and there was a 30 percent increase in quality by picking the right person, and a very expensive learning process for us was finding out human error exists!

What do translators earn?

Between $8 and $20 an hour, depending on how fast and competent they are. Right now the average text per hour is 1,200 words.

Isn't that much less than normal pay of 10-15 cents a word?

Our idea is that with our superpower translator, you do way more words. A translator has lots of challenges: you spend 50 percent of their time bidding for jobs you don't get, and 50 percent of the rest of the time dealing with stupid formatting. We help you be much more efficient, like a spellchecker on steroids, so you focus on the things you are really good at. We are going to pay less per word but in the end, you are going to make more money.

What went right, compared with your other ventures?

The team was right: five people aligned around a problem they had a lot of expertise on. In 2014 we raised $400,000 here in Portugal, we went to Y Combinator and on demo day we raised $1.5m.

Would you recommend an accelerator program like Y Combinator?

It was incredibly useful. I did AlphaLab in Pittsburgh, SURGE in Texas, we were also selected for Seedcamp in Europe, and I was a mentor at the Lisbon Challenge. YC is definitely the best. The biggest benefit is the philosophy and no bullshit approach. All of the partners have been successful founders. They will make a lot of money but they are not doing it for that – they feel it is fundamentally important great businesses are created. YC is about hard work: no silver bullets or shortcuts. For three months, you focus on the business, build customers or product. We rented an apartment with two bedrooms, four of us in one room, Sofia in another, and the living room was the office. You wake up and spend 16 hours working until you're about to sleep, all together, all the time, for three months.

So you five were like the Spice Girls?

Like the Spice Girls – yes! If things are going to go wrong, they are going to go wrong really fast. If your co-founders are going to get on your nerves, you're going to find out. That's the philosophy: fail fast. And the other is don't talk to investors until the end. YC is the only investor we have that says: focus on becoming profitable. The best way of knowing if you are producing something valuable is if people pay for it.

How much investment have you raised?

We have $3.1m and are in the process of closing a series A [the first significant round of investment]. We are doing $100,000 of revenue a month, but we have expenses. Break even, we think, is going to come next year. We have 26 people here and Sofia's in the US. Anybody can register to be a translator and do tests and once you're good enough you are paid.

What does the customer pay?

We can go down to 3c a word. Right now we are really good at conversational content and focused on that, specifically in customer service. We have a product to let people provide services in email support in twenty-two different languages, getting a translation in five to twenty minutes. On customer service, we have a 60 percent margin.

How do you ensure quality?

We deduct marks for errors in fluency, grammar. Each error has a certain number of points and you get a quality score. 80/100 is okay for an email. Emotional content needs 98 or 99. A lot of our translations come out better than the original.

What have you done wrong?

When we started, we would break text apart, send it to people and didn't have a senior translator at the end. We look back and think that was horrible. We should have spent more time in the beginning talking to people in the translation space. It also took us too long to focus on what we were good at. We tried to do everything in translation for a year.

I hear you all surf together?

Startups can have technical debt, doing things fast that you will have to correct. But you can't accumulate emotional debt with co-founders: it's easy not to talk things through. Surf did that for us. You go out and do this physical activity that demands all your attention, and afterwards you feel relaxed and can have those conversations. It reminds me of another thing that people do. Until recently, every week vans [we had hired] would come and take us to the beach, people who wanted to go in the water would go in the water, and after we would have sangria. Now we do it once a month.

What are you focused on right now?

There's a lot of technology to build, reducing the cost per word to a point where that becomes meaningless, and creating a replicable model to scale without becoming an agency: our goal is to become the world's translation layer.

What about for your translators?

We have this crazy vision. Our goal is for our office entrance to become a wireless café next year with free coffee for our translators. Why don't we also have a building at every office where they can stay? Instead of backpacking for a year, why not Unbabel? Our vision is Unbabel boats, trains, an Unbabel card so you don't need currency… The goal is to create a true community, remove language barriers and connect cultures.

[About]   Unbabel is a speed translation service for customer services teams, using a combination of artificial intelligence and international translators. It delivers translations in five to twenty minutes, aiming to be 'the world's translation layer.'

[Links]   Web: **unbabel.com** Facebook: **unbabel** Twitter: **@Unbabel** Instagram: **Unbabel**

What are you reading?
Snow Crash by Neal Stephenson and
Neuromancer by William Gibson.

What are you listening to?
Bossa nova.

What's your favourite app?
Slack.

What are your work essentials?
A laptop, internet connection and plenty of caffeine.

What skill do you wish you had?
I wish I could do hand prestidigitation [conjuring tricks].
Sleight of hand can be very useful!

What time do you wake up each morning?
7:30am.

João Romão

CEO / GetSocial

It's 9am, and João Romão has been in his office for two hours. The 27-year-old entrepreneur is creating a quick survey for 200 contacts and customers of his analytics website, which helps publishers and marketing companies monitor and make the most of viral content. This survey shows how far his business has come: he researches customer demand instead of wasting months on bright ideas nobody may buy. And even if the smart MacBook he's using is a couple of years old, the last founder standing at GetSocial at least has a working laptop. Plus a salary, and a firm that is on the point of turning a profit. That's a long way up from his lowest point...

How did you start as an entrepreneur?
As a student, you're always looking for sources of income. In 2006, there wasn't an easy way to have a website without knowing how to code, and you would still need a web server. One of my colleagues from an engineering course at ISCTE in Lisbon, Bruno Matias, and I started discussing this. The first project, Netcko.com, allowed everyone a free, quality hosting service to host their websites and, in exchange, they showed our ads via Google AdSense. I wouldn't call it a company, although it made money.

That's a good start.
For two 19-year-olds, €500 a month was a basic income. When I went to study in Brazil for the fourth year of my course and Bruno went to work at Deloitte, we gave the operation to a Brazilian company.

After a year abroad, you joined Novabase as a consultant in 2011. What then?
I didn't last long. My colleagues [Pedro Moura and João Gomes] and I were always talking about this problem. When someone was about to give or receive a present, it often resulted in a gift card, pair of socks or an unwanted gift. We ended up doing a survey of 2,000 people, and found 70 percent had problems finding the perfect gift. We saw some stats from the US stating that 40 percent of the gifts given in the previous year were not used, sent back or thrown away. We started our first startup, Wishareit.

What does that mean?
Wish-share-it. When we created it, we thought: this is brilliant. Then we understood that no-one gets it! It was definitely our problem. The goal for Wishareit was to help people find the perfect gifts. You would log in with your Facebook account, we would pull your friends' data in and you could quickly start connecting products with people. It was basically a collaborative wish list where people could give and receive recommendations, then use the 'buy' button to give a gift.

If someone clicked, you would get a commission?
Exactly. The problem was our audience was people of 21, who normally get together to give a

193

gift. Most times, people would use the platform to find a gift and go to a store to buy it. Our conversion was very low and we never made much money. So that was a poor business experience.

You raised some capital, though?

We raised about €30,000 from business angels, put in some money from friends, family and ourselves but that paid for the infrastructure and people working with us. We got to seven people outside the three founders, but the founders never got a single paycheck. It was us plus the business angels' money funding the whole business. It closed in May/June 2013, and pivoted to GetSocial.

What were the main lessons?

One of our mistakes was being extremely focused on building the product not the business. We were blind about growing the number of users and engagement. A company must make money or have explosive growth. We were growing quite fast but not venture capital fast. Without that growth, you need to turn to revenue and without that revenue the company fails. We grew the team, which we definitely couldn't afford. And it's not very cool to go two years without a salary. It's ok to test a product, hypothesis or business, but you want to do that in three to five months and have very specific goals. We lived that dream for two years and it was exhausting: financially, emotionally, physically.

Was there a wake-up call?

The wake-up call was when I had to work from my parents' home because I didn't have any money to buy a travel pass. My PC broke. I emailed some of my LinkedIn contacts asking if anyone had a PC to share with me, because I was embarrassed to ask my parents for more money. The options were closing the business or trying to make quick money out of it. We went for the latter and tried to pitch Wishareit as a service for companies in June 2013. Instead of building a product, we just did a presentation, and had some initial contacts that were quite positive. It was quite quick from the initial idea to the point we got money. Faber Ventures and Portugal Ventures put up the seed round of €630,000 in September 2013. The day I closed the deal, I went to have lunch to celebrate with some friends, and discovered I had just cents in my account. I had to ask somebody else to pay. But we funded GetSocial.

How did you get this name?

We didn't want the same mistake of a wordplay, started thinking how we were helping our customers get more social, so GetSocial was the obvious and available option. The goal was to help e-commerce companies have collaborative mechanisms on their websites to increase engagement and ultimately sales. And that failed as well.

But it failed faster?

We developed a simple product in five months, then reality kicked in when we started to sell. I contacted more than 150 companies but got the same 'no's. Mainly: 'you are doing stuff that's nice to have but will ultimately drive my customers away from buying.' We realized we weren't going to get anywhere and said: let's ditch it and make something people want. This was in May 2014. With this came an unpleasant situation. Two of the four initial founders left [Moura and Gomes].

> *"It's easier to build something, get people in the funnel using that product and let them say what you should build next."*

João Romão

Was it personal?

It was a mix of disagreements and people being very tired. We had been failing for three years. It's exhausting. In September, we launched a new product, aimed at end websites with one feature that had worked from the previous two companies: people sharing their thoughts. Our goal was to help websites get more traffic, insights and engagement out of social media. We built the initial features around what the initial users were telling us would be useful and what they would be willing to pay for. From September to the end of the year, we got 1000 websites using us [free].

Why?

It's easier to build something, get people in the funnel using that product and let them say what you should build next. Today we give publishers real-time insight on what content is becoming viral on social media. This provides data, and what we want to provide is automation, less work on their side for more results. Now we are suggesting that if we have the intelligence to say this is a story you should be pushing on Facebook, why don't we do that for you and make you a better professional with our help?

So you're sending a survey from this nice laptop to ask them if they'd like this service?

The laptop's old, but it's good. Two years ago, we'd probably spend two months building this feature then seeing if anyone wants it. Now I try to discover the best way to sell by communicating to a daily problem, and most importantly discovering whether and how they'd be willing to pay for this feature.

What's happened since September 2014?

We have grown to 100,000 websites using us and 750 paying customers, including Adobe, Sky Italy, Forbes and FedEx, paying from $9 a month to $4,000. We started with sharing tools for websites, buttons that allow you to share content on social media, which have little value: we can charge $9 a month. Mid-2015 we wanted to add value and discovered people didn't know what happened after the share. People also stopped sharing via the button but used copy-and-paste. Last year we launched our analytics platform at $99 for the first half million visits, which scales with volume. We're developing more insights on how people are sharing content and providing companies a 'virality' alert when things are picking up, via email or Slack notification. With that, we charge from $299 to $4,000 a month.

Have you raised more money?

We are raising now, but still living out of the first investment. I got quite conservative about the way I spend money. There may have been times where we could have hired more people to get us to a goal faster. But it's super likely that in two or three months we will be making more money than we spend: we are at break-even point, which gives you comfort and validation. We need money to scale, and that's wholly different.

And this time you've been taking a salary? How do you decide what it is?

The same way I decide everyone else's, which is posing the question: how much do you need for money not to be an issue in your daily life? In Lisbon, anything higher than €1,200 a month is more than okay. If you're in London, it doesn't cover your rent. That's why I try to have people here and in Porto, which is even less expensive. I'll go wherever I need to go while maintaining the product team in Lisbon.

How important is it to get the right people?

Very important. Any company from the UK, Ireland, France and Germany can say: 'We like you: here's three times your salary'. It's even more difficult to have your team committed.
Apart from António Gorgulho, the first employee who is now the CTO since all the other founders left, everyone else was recommended by others. We favor an ability for structured thinking. We also like to maintain the age as low as possible.

Why?

I think it's important to have a similar pace and I always say we should spend the most time possible together in a work day. I'm a very early riser and get to the office at 7 a.m. We get the whole team – five full-time plus two interns – working together for seven to nine hours.

Any advice to other people starting up here?

First, congratulations for coming to Lisbon. I would rather a twenty-hour-a-day week in a sunny city, with good, affordable food and low rent, over Berlin or London. If you're doing a product or service, don't test your hypothesis with only Portuguese companies – tie in with the correct market so you don't have surprises. One of the things I don't like about Portuguese business etiquette is that the Portuguese don't like to say no. If a German doesn't like your business, he will say: thank you for your time, I'm not interested. Portuguese people will keep you in the loop, inviting you to meetings and, nine months later, say they don't quite have the budget. They do. They're just not interested.

You've learnt plenty of business lessons, but are you still exhausted?

I work on that. The sad/happy thing is that my girlfriend – we've lived together for three years – is a consultant at Deloitte and has the same workload or even higher. It's getting home at 10pm too tired to have dinner, having soup together, talking about the day, going to bed, waking up the next day. Even at GetSocial, I had some dark times, going to sleep at night tired and waking at 3am worrying about the next day. For me, that meant getting in the shower and coming to the office, but it's not necessarily better or sustainable for your mind or body. I started taking vacations, which I didn't have for four years. I take one or two weeks a year – what, is it too low? And I stopped doing work-related stuff on the weekends.

Is an element of obsession necessary?

I think you have to make things happen, and normally that means doing as much as you can in a short period. But if I started something new, before writing a line of code, I would make a four-month plan with very specific milestones, and quit much faster if I wasn't getting there. Otherwise, you stay obsessed for six months not having any time for yourself, family or friends, and fail anyway. You have to find a healthy balance.

[About]   GetSocial tracks how people read and share content from publishers and marketing companies, helping them promote their articles via social media and turn them viral. It is used by more than 100,000 websites worldwide.

[Links]   Web: **getsocial.io** Facebook: **getsocial.io** Twitter: **@getsocial_io**

What are you reading?
Never Eat Alone by Keith Ferrazzi and Tahl Raz
Ender's Game by Orson Scott Card

What are you listening to?
Spotify tells me this is what's going on my playlists: Ramin
Djawadi, Elvis Presley, Hans Zimmer, The Bohicas.

What's your favorite app?
Sleep Cycle

What's your favourite podcast?
Hardcore History by Dan Carlin

What are your work essentials?
Google Apps + Sunrise + HubSpot + Keynote

What skill do you wish you had?
I'd love to be fluent in as many languages as possible

What time do you wake up in the morning?
Sleep Cycle tells me my average is around 06.25am

directory

Startups

Aptoide
Rua Soeiro Pereira Gomes
Lote 1 – 3º D, 1600-196
Lisbon
aptoide.com

Attentive
attentive.us

Codacy
Largo Adelino Amaro da
Costa, nº8 3º Dto
1100-006 Lisbon
codacy.com

CoolFarm
CoolFarm S.A., BizSpark, Rua
do Fogo de Santelmo, Lote
2.07.02, 1990-119 Lisbon
cool-farm.com

EatTasty
Rua da Emenda 19,
1200-169 Lisbon
eattasty.com

Hole19
Rua da Assunção 7,
1100-042 Lisbon
hole19golf.com

Landing.jobs
Rua Alexandre Herculano 2
4D, 1150-006 Lisbon
landing.jobs

Line Health
Praça Carlos Fabião,
nr 3, Esc 2, 1600-316 Lisbon
linehealth.com

Science4you
MARL - São Julião do Tojal,
Lugar do Quintanilho -
Plataforma do Rouco CC02
e CC03, 2660-421 Loures
science4youtoys.com

Talkdesk
Rua Tierno Galvan, 10 -
tower 3, 15º floor, 1070-274
talkdesk.com

Tradiio
R. Luciano Cordeiro 123,
1050-139 Lisbon
tradiio.com

Programs

Acredita Portugal
LABS Lisboa - Incubadora
de Inovação, Rua Adriano
Correia de Oliveira - 4 A,
1600 – 312
acreditaportugal.pt

Big Smart Cities
bigsmartcities.com

Building Global Innovators
Reitoria ISCTE-IUL (Building
1), Avenida das Forças
Armadas, 1649-026 Lisbon
bgi.pt

FastStart
Rua Rodrigo da Fonseca,
nº11, 1250-189, Lisbon
fabricadestartups.com

Lisbon Challenge
Avenida Casal Ribeiro 28,
1000-092 Lisbon
lisbon-challenge.com

Productized
Startup Campus, Rua Rodrigo
da Fonseca 11, 1º,
1250-189 Lisbon
productized.co

Spaces

Beta-i (incubator)
Avenida Casal Ribeiro 28,
1000-092 Lisbon
beta-i.pt

Coworklisboa
Rua Rodrigues Faria 103, LX
Factory, main building, 4th
floor, 1300-501 Lisbon
coworklisboa.pt/en

Liberdade 229
Avenida da Liberdade 229,
1250-142 Lisbon
liberdade229.com

**LINNK
(Lisbon Innovation Kluster)**
Rua Braamcamp 88,
5th floor, 1250-052 Lisbon
linnk.us

Lisbon WorkHub
Rua Amorim 2,
1950-022 Lisbon
lisbonworkhub.pt

Mouraria Creative Hub
Rua dos Lagares 23,
1100-022 Lisbon
www.cm-lisboa.pt/en/
mouraria-creative-hub

Startup Campus
Rua Rodrigo da Fonseca 11,
1250-189 Lisbon
fabricadestartups.co

Startup Lisboa
Rua da Prata 80-81,
1100-415 Lisbon
startuplisboa.com

The Surf Office
Rua de São Paulo 111,
2nd floor, 1200-275 Lisbon
thesurfoffice.com

Village Underground Lisboa
Museu da Carris, Estação de
Santo Amaro, R. 1º de Maio
103, 1300-472 Lisbon
vulisboa.com

Experts

Airbnb
airbnb.com

Bright Pixel
Rua da Emenda,
N. 19, 1200-169 Lisbon
brpx.com

EDP Inovação
Av. 24 de Julho,
12, 1249-300 Lisbon
edpstarter.com

Lisbon City Council
Iniciativa Lisboa,
Campo Grande 13 B,
1700 - 087 Lisbon
www.cm-lisboa.pt/en/
business/investor-and-
entrepreneur-support

Microsoft
Rua do Fogo de Santelmo,
Lote 2.07.02, 1990 - 110
microsoft.com

**Morais Leitão, Galvão
Teles, Soares da Silva &
Associados (MLGTS)**
Rua Castilho, 165,
1070-050 Lisbon
mlgts.pt

Santander Totta
R. Mesquita, 6,
1070-238 Lisbon
santandertotta.pt

SAP Startup Focus
SAP Portugal, Edificio 4,
Piso 3, 2740-267 Porto Salvo
startupfocus.saphana.com

**Sonae Investment
Management**
Rua da Emenda 19,
1200-169 Lisbon
sonaeim.com

Interviews

Chic by Choice
Avenida da Liberdade 230,
1250-148 Lisbon
chic-by-choice.com

Feedzai
Avenida D. Joao II, Lote
1.16.01, Piso 11,
1990-083 Lisbon
feedzai.com

GetSocial
Rua Rodrigo da Fonseca, 11,
1250-189 Lisbon
getsocial.io

Uniplaces
Rossio Train Station 17,
Largo do Duque de Cadaval,
1200-160 Lisbon
uniplaces.com

Unbabel
Rua Visconde de Santarém
67B, 1000-286 Lisbon
unbabel.com

Accountants

Deloitte
Av. Eng. Duarte Pacheco 7,
1070-100
deloitte.com/pt

KPMG
Edifício Monumental,
Avenida Praia da Vitória,
71-A, 8th floor
kpmg.com/pt

**PwC (Pricewaterhouse-
Coopers & Associados)**
Palácio Sottomayor,
Rua Sousa Martins, 1st
and 2nd floor, 1069-316
pwc.com

Radical Innovation
Madan Parque,
Rua dos Inventores,
2825-182 Caparica
radicalinnovation.pt

Banks

Activobank
Rua Garrett 68, 1200-203
activobank.pt

Banco Best
Pç Marquês de Pombal 3,
2nd floor, 1250-161
bancobest.pt

Caixa Geral de Depósitos
cgd.pt

Coffee Shops and Places with Wifi

**Bairro do Avillez
– José Avillez**
Rua Nova da Trindade 18
joseavillez.pt/en/
bairro-do-avillez

Brick Cafe
Rua de Moçambique 2
facebook.com/
BrickCafeLisboa

Café com Calma
Rua do Açúcar 10,
1950-242 Lisbon
facebook.com/
cafecomcalmamarvila

Cafe Tati
Rua Ribeira Nova 36, Lisbon
facebook.com/caféTATI

Choupana Caffé
Av. da República 25A, Lisbon
facebook.com/
Choupanacaffe

Copenhagen Coffee Lab
1200 192, R. Nova da Piedade
10, Lisbon
cphcoffeelab.pt

The Decadente
Rua de São Pedro de
Alcantara 81,
1250-238 Lisbon
thedecadente.pt/rest

Deli Delux
Avenida Infante Dom
Henrique Armazém B,
Loja 8, 1900-264
delidelux.pt

La Boulangerie
Rua do Olival, 42, 1200-739

directory

O Pão Nosso
R. Marquês Sá da Bandeira
46, 1050-149 Lisbon
facebook.com/opaonosso.pt

Tartine
R. Serpa Pinto 15A, Lisbon
tartine.pt

**Time Out Mercado
da Ribeira**
(lots of places/events
in one market)
Avenida 24 de Julho 49, 1200
timeout.com/market

Vélocité Cafe (you can
also rent a bike here)
Avenida Duque de Ávila,
Nº.120-A, Lisbon
velocitecafe.com

Expat Groups and Meetups

**British Community
Council, Lisbon**
(English speakers'
umbrella group)
bcclisbon.org

French-Upers Lisbonne
meetup.com/Meetup-
French-Start-Upers-a-
Lisbonne

Internations
internations.org

**Lisbon Casuals sports
and social club**
lisboncasuals.com

The Lisbon Players
(amateur theatre)
Rua da Estrela, nº 10,
1200-669
lisbonplayerse.com.pt

Flats and Rentals

Casa Sapo
(popular online portal)
casa.sapo.pt

HomeLovers
Rua Castilho 71,
1250-068
homelovers.pt

JLL Cobertura
Cobertura.pt

Moviinn
Rua de São Paulo 109, Lisbon
moviinn.com

Portugal Property
Avenida da Liberdade
240-4th floor, 1250-148
portugalproperty.com

Insurance Companies

Açoreana
Av. Duque d' Ávila,
171 1069-031
acoreanaseguros.pt

Allianz Seguros
allianz.pt

Fidelidade
fidelidade.pt

Incubators in the City

Fábrica de Startups
Rua Rodrigo da Fonseca 11,
1250-096
fabricadestartups.co

**LABS Lisboa – Incubadora
de Inovação**
Rua Adriano Correia de
Oliveira 4A, 1600-312
labslisboa.pt

**LISPOLIS - Centro de In-
cubação e Desenvolvimento**
Estrada do Paço do Lumiar 44
lispolis.pt

Investors in the City

Caixa Capital
Rua Barata Salgueiro, 33,
1st floor, 1269-057
caixacapital.pt

Faber Ventures
Time Out Mercado da
Ribeira, Av. 24 de Julho 49
faber-ventures.com

LC Ventures
Rua Casal Ribeiro, 28,
2nd floor, 1000-092
lcventures.pt

Portugal Ventures
Edifício Arcis, Rua Ivone Silva
6, 12th floor, 1050-124
Portugalventures.pt

Schilling Capital
Campo Grande, 28, 3º B,
1700-093 Lisbon
shillingcapital.com

Language Schools in the City

**CESA Languages
Abroad**
Rua Actor Taborda, 55,
1st floor 1000-007
cesalanguages.com

CIAL centro de linguas
Rua Actor Taborda, 55,
1st floor. 1000-007
cial.pt

Eurolingua Institute
eurolingua.com

Linguas&Linguas
ESCOLA DE LÍNGUAS,
Praça Luís Camões, 22 -
2ºdto, 1200-243
languagelisboa.net

Phone Companies

MEO
meo.pt

NOS
nos.pt

Vodafone
vodafone.pt

Public Transport

Carris
Customer care at Avenida
Duque D´Ávila, nº 12,
1000-140
carris.transporteslisboa.pt

Comboios de Portugal (CP)
Calçada do Duque, 20,
1249-109
cp.pt

Fertagus
Pragal station, door 23,
2805-333 Almada
fertagus.pt

Metro
Complexo de Carnide,
Estrada da Pontinha,
1600-582
metro.transporteslisboa.pt

Startup Events

BREAK Lisboa
meetup.com/BREAKlx

Coworklisboa
(first Wednesday of
the month brunch)
LX Factory, Rua Rodrigues
Faria 103, main building,
4th floor, 1300-501
coworklisboa.pt

GRID networking and drinks
Rua Rodrigo da Fonseca nº11,
1250-189
fabricadestartups.co

Incubadoras Lisboa
(city council collective of
investors/places/spaces)
incubadoraslisboa.pt

Lisbon Investment Summit
lis-summit.com

Startup Weekend Lisbon
lisbon.startupweekend.org
or up.co/communities/
portugal/lisbon

#TGIF
Avenida Casal Ribeiro 28,
1000-092
beta-i.pt

**Web Summit
2016, 2017, 2018**
Feira Internacional de Lisboa
and Meo Arena, Rua Bojador,
1998-010 Santa Maria
dos Olivais
websummit.comnet

Important Government Offices

AICEP Portugal Global
(economic agency)
Avenida 5 de Outubro 101,
1050-051 Lisbon
portugalglobal.pt

Empresa na Hora
(speedy business
set-up scheme)
Rua Augusto Pina, 21-RC
Loja A, 1500 – 065 Lisbon
empresanahora.pt

Incubadoras de Lisboa
incubadoraslisboa.pt

Iniciativa Lisboa
(council one-stop-shop)
Campo Grande, 13, Lisbon
cm-lisboa.pt/investir

Invest Lisboa (investment
promotional agency)
Rua das Portas de Santo
Antão 89, 1169-022 Lisbon
Investlisboa.com

**Lisbon Business
Connections**
Rua das Portas de Santo
Antão, 89 - 1169-022
lisbonconnections.pt

Portal da Empresa
(Portuguese,
English, Spanish)
portaldaempresa.pt

**Portuguese Institute
of Industrial Property**
(to register patents
or trademarks)
NPI, Serviço de Atendimento,
Campo das Cebolas,
1149-035
marcasepatentes.pt

SEF
(immigration/border service)
Avenida António Augusto
de Aguiar 20, 1069-119
sef.pt

Startup Portugal
startupportugal.com

glossary

A

Accelerator
An organization or program that offers advice and resources to help small businesses grow

Acqui-hire
Buying out a company based on the skills of its staff rather than its service or product

Angel Investment
[FUNDING STAGE]
Outside funding with shared ownership equity

ARR
Accounting (or average) rate of return: calculation generated from net income of the proposed capital investment

B

B2B
(business-to-business)
The exchange of services, information and/or products from a business to a business

B2C
(business-to-consumer)
The exchange of services, information and/or products from a business to a consumer

BOM
(Bill of Materials)
The list of the parts or components required to build a product

Bootstrap
[FUNDING STAGE]
Self-funded, without outside investment

Bridge Loan
A short-term loan taken out from between two weeks and three years pending arrangement of longer-term financing

Burn Rate
The amount of money a startup spends

Business Angel
An experienced entrepreneur or professional who provides starting or growth capital for promising startups

C

C-level
Chief position

Canvas Business Model
A template for developing new or documenting existing business models

Cap Table
An analysis of the founders' and investors' percentage of ownership, equity dilution, and value of equity in each round of investment

CMO
Chief marketing officer

Cold-Calling
The solicitation of potential customers who were not anticipating such an interaction

Convertible Note/Loan
A type of short-term debt often used by seed investors to delay establishing a valuation for the startup until a later round of funding or milestone

Co-Working
A shared working environment

CPA
Cost per action

CPC
Cost per click

Cybersecurity
The body of technologies, processes and practices designed to protect networks, computers, programs and data from attack, damage or unauthorized access

D

Dealflow
Term for investors to refer to the rate at which they receive business proposals

Diluting
A reduction in the ownership percentage of a share of stock caused by the issuance of new shares

E

Elevator Pitch
A short summary used to quickly define a product or idea

Exit
A way to transition the ownership of a company to another company

F

Fintech
Financial technology

Flex Desk
Shared desks in a space where co-workers are free to move around and sit wherever they like.

I

Incubator
Facility established to nurture young startup firms during their early months or years

IP (Intellectual Property)
Intangible property that is the result of creativity, such as patents, copyrights, etc.

IPO
(Initial Public Offering)
The first time a company's stock is offered for sale to the public

L

Later-Stage
More mature startups/companies

M

M&A
(Mergers and Acquisitions)
A merger is a combination of two companies to form a new company, while an acquisition is the purchase of one company by another in which no new company is formed.

MAU
Monthly active user

MVP
Minimum viable product

P

Pitch Deck
A short version of a business plan presenting key figures

PR-Kit (Press Kit)
Package of pictures, logos and descriptions of your services

R

Runtime
The amount of time a startup has survived

S

SAAS
Software as a service

Scaleup
Company that has already validated its product in a market, and is economically sustainable

Seed Funding
[FUNDING STAGE]
First round, small, early-stage investment from family members, friends, banks or an investor

Seed Investor
An investor focusing on the seed round

Seed Round
The first round of funding

Series A/B/C/D
The name of funding rounds coming after the seed stage

Shares
The amount of the company that belongs to someone

Startup
Companies under three years old, in the growth stage and becoming profitable (if not already)

SVP
Senior Vice President

T

Term Sheet/Letter of Intent
The document between an investor and a startup including the conditions for financing (commonly non-binding)

U

UX
(User experience design)
The process of enhancing user satisfaction by improving the usability, accessibility, and pleasure provided in the interaction between the user and the product.

Unicorn
A company worth over $1 billion

V

VC (Venture Capital)
[FUNDING STAGE]
Outside venture capital investment from a pool of investors in a venture capital firm in return for equity

VC
Venture capitalist

Vesting
Employee rights to employer-provided assets over time, which gives the employee an incentive to perform well and remain with the company

With thanks to our content sponsors

airbnb

SONAE IM

edp

brpx Bright Pixel

Morais Leitão
Galvão Teles
Soares da Silva

Santander

About the Guide

Based on the idea of a traditional guidebook to carry with you everywhere, the guides are made to inspire a generation to become more successful entrepreneurs through case-stories, advice and expert knowledge. Useful for when you start a project or business, the guide gives insight on where to go, who to talk to and what not to miss from the local people who know the city best.

How we make the guides:

To ensure an accurate and trustworthy guide every time, we team up with a local city partner, ideally an established organization with experience in the local startup scene, who conducts a general call out to the local community to nominate startups, co-working spaces, founders, incubators and established businesses through an online submission form. These submissions are narrowed down to the top fifty selected companies and individuals. The local advisory board then votes anonymously for the final selection to represent the range of industries and startup stories in the city. The local team, in close collaboration with our editorial and design team in Berlin, then organize and conduct the interviews, photoshoots and research necessary, using local journalists and photographers. All content is then reviewed, edited and approved by the Startup Guide team in Berlin and Copenhagen HQ who are together responsible from then on through to design, layout and final print production.

Who makes the guides:

Sissel Hansen – Founder / CEO
Thomas Nymark Horsted – Co-Founder / COO

Jenna van Uden – Editor
Maurice Redmond – Art Director
Senay Boztas – Writer
Laurence Currie-Clark – Copyeditor

Daniela Carducci – Photo Editor
Sanjini Redmond – Illustrator
Anka Cybis – Graphic Designer
Emilie Delarge – Graphic Designer
Sofi Sitha Natarajah – Head of Marketing
Erik Hebbe – Retail and Sales Assistant
Matteo Cossu – Content Programmer

Contact us at info@startupeverywhere.com if you would like us to come to your city.

WHERE NEXT?